D0906861

HUM
428.34
Y65s

Springboards

Communication Starters

Richard Yorkey

Alta Book Center Publishers—San Francisco
14 Adrian Court ◆ Burlingame, California 94010 USA

The Author Richard Yorkey taught English and trained teachers of English to speakers of other languages at the American University of Beirut, Lebanon; Concordia University in Montreal; and St. Michael's College in Winooski, Vermont, where *Springboards* was developed and tested.

Acknowledgements

"You Be the Judge" adapted and used with permission from the Curtis Publishing Company © 1979.

"Story Pictures," *Saturday Evening Post* covers reproduced with permission from the Curtis Publishing Company © 1947, 1953, 1958, 1959, 1960.

"Picture Gallery," photographs: p. 8, Compliments of Schering Corporation; p. 9, Courtesy of Talbot F. Hamlin; p. 10, Courtesy of American Bankers Association; p. 11, © Corbis; p. 12, Claire Smith photo.

Other illustrations by Tom Leamon and Larry Matteson, with the exception of select tool drawings on page 21, drawn by Natesh Daniel.

Acquisitions Editor: Aaron Berman

Content and Production Editors: Raissa Nina Burns and Jamie Ann Cross

Cover Design: Bruce Marion Design

Interior Design: Leigh McLellan Design

Icon Design: Natesh Daniel

Alta Book Center Publishers
14 Adrian Court
Burlingame, California 94010
Website: www.altaesl.com • Email: info@altaesl.com
Phone: 800 ALTA/ESL or 650.692.1285 (International)
Fax: 800 ALTA/FAX or 650.692.4654 (International)
ISBN 1-882483-93-6
Library of Congress Control Number 2004101330

Introduction

Communication is increasingly recognized as an important goal in English classes for speakers of other languages. Communication in this context means more than simply sitting around and talking in what is usually called a conversation class. Rather, it means an exchange of interesting, often necessary information. This exchange is stimulated and fostered by activities.

Second-language teachers are unusually busy people, however, and they frequently do not have the time to prepare the wide range of materials needed for such communication activities. For second-language classes of a semester or longer, in particular, teachers require a collection of classroom-tested materials that provide a range and variety of interesting, motivating communication activities that students will enjoy while at the same time increasing their skill and facility with the language.

Springboards is intended to fill this need. Each photocopiable activity presents students with a task that can best be solved by interaction between students. Many of the tasks are open-ended and students are asked to defend and justify their responses. Others help them gain basic skills: again, students are asked to discuss how they solved the problems and to share learning and study techniques with their classmates. All of these activities have been tried out in second-language classes that range from low-intermediate to advanced, with students of various ages and language backgrounds.

I would like to thank my colleagues at the International Student Program of St. Michael's College, Winooski, Vermont, who gave me valuable feedback during their trial use of various activities. Some of my TESOL graduate students at St. Michael's also offered helpful comments, and I'm especially pleased to acknowledge the insightful criticism of Mary Plante and Deryn Verity. Finally, I am happy to thank Talbot F. Hamlin and Elly Schottman for their unusual pedagogical perspective, their sensible suggestions, and their careful editing of a complicated collection of diverse activities.

—*Richard Yorkey*

Contents

To the Teacher

Springboards consists of nine units; each containing activities designed to foster communication skills and provide practice in using them. A special section presents exercises to help students use the various parts of their telephone directory. These exercises build student confidence in communicating by telephone. *Springboards* is adaptable for use from low-intermediate to advanced levels.

As a teacher, you play a vital role in helping students profit from the *Springboards* activities. In particular, you can help in establishing a variety of viable communication patterns in the classroom. Most of the pages are designed to be worked on by pairs or small groups of students. It is important to make sure that both members of a pair, or all members of a group, participate. Pair and group work also provides an excellent vehicle for peer teaching, since not all students have the same body of knowledge, and communication activities of the kind presented here encourage students to share their individual expertise. You will wish to see that student pairing and small group composition change frequently in order to allow for maximum practice in communicating with a variety of other persons.

The exercise pages have instructions written directly to the student. It is important, however, for you to go over each of these sets of directions with the students. Some of the activities require close teacher supervision and control. A few require you to provide all the directions to the students.

Springboards is designed to encourage communication, particularly oral communication. On nearly every activity, students work together. As a result, classrooms can be expected to be noisy! When groups or pairs are concentrating on an activity, you may occasionally need to ask them to be quiet; be sure, in doing so, that you do not destroy the spontaneity that true communication produces. Many activities ask students to support or justify their answers. Give students the opportunity to do so at length, if this is their inclination, and draw out those students whose responses are incomplete or so terse as to be unintelligible.

Springboards is designed to be just what its name implies: a series of activities to get students "into the swim" of communicating in English. Encourage students to follow up these activities by making up similar exercises to use with partners or groups. Encourage them to go beyond the questions posed on the "Picture Gallery" and "Story Pictures" pages, and to invent and use other kinds of "Getting Acquainted" activities. The more that students can communicate with each other, with you, and with the world outside the classroom, the more *Springboards* will have succeeded in its aim.

The Activities

There are eight principal kinds of activities in *Springboards* (in addition to the "Using the Telephone" section). General discussions of each activity type, with suggestions for its use, follow.

Unit 1 **Getting Acquainted** (pp. 1–6)

The general purpose of this group of exercises is to provide students with an opportunity to use English in social situations: getting acquainted with others, introducing themselves, asking and answering personal questions, and giving biographical information.

Sign on the Dotted Line (p. 2) invites students to ask and answer personal questions and learn the names of classmates. It is an especially useful "icebreaking" activity for new classes. As a follow-up to this activity, students may report their answers to the rest of the class; you can then follow these questions such as "How many like Madonna?" or "Who else was born in August?" If someone has claimed to be able to recite a poem in English (item 9), be sure to give him or her a chance to do so (or to politely decline the invitation).

Family Tree (p. 3) provides an opportunity for students to ask and answer family questions and review the names of family relationships. You may wish to sketch your own family tree (or part of it) on the board, writing a list of the names that appear on the page. (At this point it is probably best to avoid cousins, nieces, and nephews.) There are two ways in which the page can be used. Either (1) have the student fill out his or her partner's family tree or, if this requires more language than students have, (2) have the student fill out his or her own family tree. The first of these methods should be used if possible, since it requires students to ask questions to which they don't already know the answers, and to speak clearly enough for their partners to understand. When the family trees are completed, students can ask each other questions about particular family members. For additional practice, each partner may ask to hear the life story of one of these family members, using questions which, depending on the proficiency of the class, may have been carefully structured and rehearsed; after the interview, the student can write a brief biographical sketch of the person.

Opinion Poll (p. 4) gives additional practice in asking and answering questions, helps students organize information, and reviews and reinforces the difference between fact and opinion. When presenting the exercise, be sure that students understand what an opinion poll is and why such polls are used. Then either ask students to make up two questions of their own or give them questions to ask. In either case, be sure that a variety of questions are included, and that they are not questions that can be answered with a simple "yes" or "no." Be sure also that the questions ask for opinions, not knowledge of facts; if students are unsure of the difference between fact and opinion, review it with them. While students are polling their classmates, check to see that they understand the process of tallying answers. As a follow-up, especially with advanced students, you might suggest continuing the polling outside of the class or school and organizing results in terms of the percent of the polled group giving each response.

Interview (p. 5). This activity asks questions of a somewhat more personal nature than the earlier ones, and also asks students to go beyond simple answers and tell "why." Students get to know each other better through the sharing of memories, hopes, and preferences. After students have completed their interviews, you may wish to have them write brief biographical sketches of their interviewees.

Timeline (p. 6). In this activity, students ask (and tell) about important events in their lives. Be sure that students are paired with different partners from those interviewed in "Sign on the Dotted Line," "Family Tree," and "Interview." This activity provides the opportunity to review time and tense—the past tense *ago*, and the present perfect with *since* (plus a time point) and *for* (plus a time span). The procedure is spelled out on the activity page. First the student interviews his/her partner, using previously designed questions, then he/she chooses five dates and events and writes them on the time line. When this is completed, each student should discuss with his/her partner why the particular dates and events were chosen. Students may then wish, as a follow-up, to make more extensive timelines of their own lives.

Unit 2 **Picture Gallery** (pp. 7–12)

These activities provide practice in convergent and divergent thinking, contribute to group interaction, and require students to present and defend a personal opinion. Each activity presents a photograph of a person and asks questions about it. There are no "right" answers to the questions in the context of this exercise; any answer that students can support or defend is to be considered "right." These activities are to be done in groups of three or four students. The task of the group is to come to some agreement that each member of the group can defend to the other groups. No more than ten minutes should be allowed for group discussion and decisions.

Unit 3 **Memory Skills** (pp. 13–24)

This series of exercises will help students strengthen their memory skills. Students study a picture, a word list, or a chart for several minutes, using a given memory technique. They then test their recall by turning the page and answering questions or reproducing the material studied. (The memory activities may also be useful in building vocabulary.)

Summer Day (p. 15). With low-intermediate classes, you may want to discuss the scene and review some of the vocabulary. All students should study the picture for two or three minutes. They should first think about the entire scene, then carefully note all the details, moving from left to right. At the end of the time limit, students turn the page and answer the questions. The second picture (p. 16) is used in a similar manner, but in this instance students make up questions about it to ask a partner.

Lists (p. 17) presents a classic memorizing task: learning a list of words. Explain that it is easier to memorize words that are meaningfully organized than words listed at random. These twenty words might be made more meaningful by grouping them in some way (household things, food and drink, emotions, etc.) or by relating them in a story sequence. An alternate way to present these pages is to give no clues at all before students learn the list, then discuss methods (including those above) and follow this with a second list, so students can discover whether using a meaningful organization does in fact make memorizing easier.

The Human Skeleton (p. 19). Proceed according to the directions on the first page. Let students work in pairs and quiz each other. Then have students turn the page and work individually, writing the names of as many of the bones as possible.

Tool Shop (p. 21). Working in pairs, students can help each other memorize the names and spellings of these tools by quizzing each other. Remind them to concentrate on the tool itself and its characteristic features, not its position on the page. Pronounce the names of the tools for the students and encourage discussion of each tool's use, then give student pairs five minutes to study the page. At the end of that time, have students turn the page and write the names of the tools. If you wish, this may also be done in pairs.

The Zodiac (p. 23). In this activity, students must memorize three related items for each of the twelve groups of the Zodiac. Explain the Zodiac if needed. Have students work in pairs, both while memorizing the items and while taking the quiz. Some hints for learning the symbols are on the page.

Unit 4 Crossword Puzzles (pp. 25–41)

The puzzles in this book can best be solved by pairs of students working together. The puzzles reinforce vocabulary and structures of several kinds. The last puzzle is solved by first completing a cloze-type exercise, then entering the words in the proper places on the puzzle; it should be done in this order, although a certain amount of checking back and forth between the passage and the puzzle is inevitable.

Unit 5 You Be the Judge (pp. 43–48)

These are all genuine cases, adapted from *You Be the Judge* by Ashley Halsey, Jr. (Fawcett, 1961). The cases were tried before a judge and without a jury. State laws, not federal laws, governed the decisions. Although there is an "answer" for each case (the actual decision of the judge trying it—see the Answer Key), this is less important than each student's statement of his or her reasons for deciding for one party or other.

Unit 6 It's Only Logical (pp. 49–54)

These activities require close reading skills, logical analysis, and, for discussion and explanation in class, control of conditional sentences and modal auxiliaries. They are best used individually. When a student thinks he or she has solved the puzzle, he/she can share the answer with another student. Real interaction occurs between the pair when their answers disagree. It may be useful in some instances to sketch the "grid" on the board and ask a student to explain the solution to the rest of the class. Patterns of conditional sentences can be written on the board for review and focused practice.

Unit 7 **Story Pictures** (pp. 55–66)

The five "Story Pictures" are all reproductions of Norman Rockwell paintings for covers of the *Saturday Evening Post*. Like the "Picture Gallery" exercises, these pages are designed to promote both convergent and divergent thinking. They also develop picture analysis skills, attention to details, and the ability to go beyond literal facts and interpret present actions and emotions and predict future ones. Most importantly, they provide opportunities for students to communicate their findings and interpretations to the class either in oral reports or in writing. Each of the "Story Pictures" has three sets of activities. In general, the A set can be used with low-intermediate students, the B set with intermediate to advanced students, and the C set with advanced. Tell each student which activities to use and whether to report orally or in writing. Depending on your class, you may need to develop concepts and vocabulary before assigning the activities. This will be especially true with the last two (*Looking In, Looking Out* and *The Verdict*).

Unit 8 **Classes and Categories** (pp. 67–70)

This classic parlor game is a useful way for students to review vocabulary. In the first two games, the categories and letters are given to the students; in the third game, the letters are given but students choose their own categories. (In further games, if you wish to use them, students may choose both the letters and the categories.) The game can be played individually or in groups of two or three.

Allow students a set time (more than five minutes leads to restlessness) to fill in the words. Allowing the use of an English-English dictionary is pedagogically useful.

Unit 9 **Using the Telephone** (p. 79)

The four activities that deal with the telephone directory are intended to give students practice in finding and using information in this valuable resource. The material can be presented and discussed in class and then practiced as individual assignments, or it can be used as the basis for communicative exercises for paired practice. Each of the units includes a suggestion that students make up additional questions of their own to ask a partner or the class; in the case of the white pages, yellow pages, and Community Services pages, students are instructed to use their own telephone directories if possible. Encourage students to bring telephone directories to class, or provide them yourself. (Your local telephone company may be willing to cooperate by giving you several copies for class use.)

Getting Acquainted

Sign on the Dotted Line

Family Tree

Opinion Poll

Interview

Timeline

Sign on the Dotted Line

Directions: Move around the room and talk with your classmates. Try to find someone who fits each of the following descriptions. (Make up your own descriptions for items 11–15.) When you find a person who fits one of the descriptions, ask that person to sign his or her name on the dotted line next to that description.

Find someone who . . .

has the same initials as yours.   1. ....

was born in August.   2. ....

is one of six children.   3. ....

can speak four languages.   4. ....

has visited New York City.   5. ....

doesn't like cats.   6. ....

can play the guitar.   7. ....

is older than you.   8. ....

can recite a poem in English.   9. ....

likes Madonna.   10. ....

_____   11. ....

_____   12. ....

_____   13. ....

_____   14. ....

_____   15. ....

*This activity will help you learn more
about the people in your class.*

Family Tree

* *

Directions: A family tree shows how members of a family are related. It shows the grandparents, the parents, the aunts and uncles, and the brothers and sisters in a family.

Your teacher will tell you how to fill out this family tree.

The Family Tree of

_____

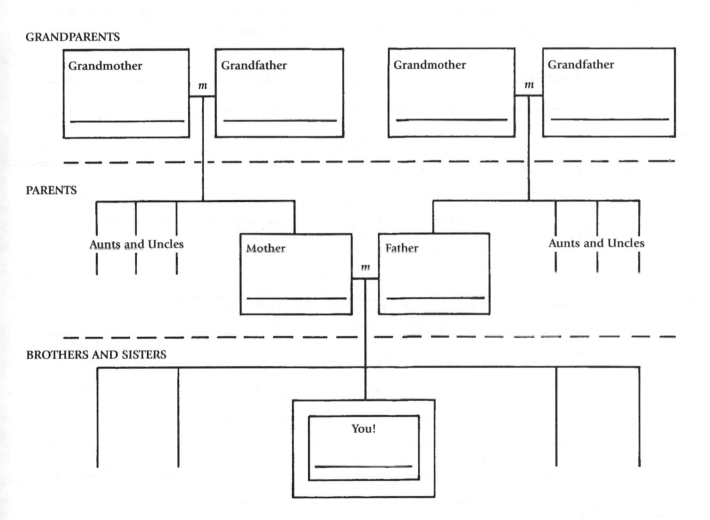

Opinion polling is big business in the United States. Almost every day you read stories in the newspaper showing how people feel about something or somebody. Here's a chance to take a poll of your own.

Opinion Poll

● ●

Directions: Take an opinion poll of students in your class. Think of two questions to ask, or use questions your teacher suggests. Remember, your questions must ask for an opinion about something: what each person thinks or feels about an issue, or what he or she likes best. Begin each question with one of these words: *Who, What, When, How, Which, Why.*

Write your questions at the top of the two columns on this page. Then ask at least twelve people in your class to answer the questions. Write the answers in the columns. Make marks next to each answer to show how many people gave that opinion.

Question 1: _____   **Question 2:** _____

_____   _____

Answer	Number of People	Answer	Number of People
_____	____	_____	____
_____	____	_____	____
_____	____	_____	____
_____	____	_____	____
_____	____	_____	____
_____	____	_____	____
_____	____	_____	____
_____	____	_____	____
_____	____	_____	____
_____	____	_____	____
_____	____	_____	____
_____	____	_____	____

When you have all your answers, arrange the answers for each question in order, listing the most common answer first (the one given by the largest number of people). Then report the results of your opinion poll to the class.

Interview

Directions: Find an interview partner. You will interview your partner and your partner will interview you. Ask your partner questions to find out the information below.

Be ready to talk about what you have learned in the interview.

Name of Interview Partner: _____

1. Present address and telephone number: _____

   _____

2. Schools attended: _____

   _____

3. Number and ages of brothers and sisters: _____

   _____

4. Favorite color and why: _____

   _____

5. Favorite food and why: _____

   _____

6. Favorite free-time activity and why: _____

   _____

7. Favorite place to be and why: _____

   _____

8. Best childhood memory: _____

   _____

9. Most important event in your life: _____

   _____

10. Hope for the future: _____

    _____

Timeline

• •

Directions: What are the important dates in your partner's life? Why are these dates so important? Before you begin the interview, think of some questions that should produce an interesting interview. For example: "How long have you lived in this city?" "What were you doing five years ago?" "How has your life changed since then? Why?" Write at least three other questions to use in your interview.

_____

_____

_____

_____

_____

_____

_____

_____

During your interview, take notes on a separate piece of paper. Write down each year and event your partner mentions.

After the interview, choose five dates from your notes and write them on the timeline. Write the dates in the parentheses. The earliest date should be at the bottom and the most recent date at the top. Then, on the lines, briefly describe the events that make each date important.

The Timeline of _____

(Today)   **Important Events**

_____

_____

_____

(   ) _____

_____

_____

_____

_____

(   ) _____

_____

_____

_____

(   ) _____

_____

_____

_____

(   ) _____

_____

_____

_____

(   ) _____

_____

_____

(Birth)

Picture Gallery

Tea Time

Strawberries

Midnight

On the Phone

What's Going On?

Here's a picture for you to look at. A picture can tell you a lot about a person. What do you feel you can learn about a person from his or her picture?

Tea Time

· ·

Directions: Discuss the woman in this picture with several classmates. Try to agree on answers to the questions at the bottom of the page. Write short answers in the blanks, and be prepared to tell the class why you answered as you did.

What nationality do you think this woman is?_____

Is she married, single, widowed, or divorced? _____

Is she poor, middle income, or wealthy? _____

Who do you think she is having tea with? _____

What are they talking about? _____

Would you like to meet her? Why or why not? _____

Here's a picture for you to look at. A picture can tell you a lot about a person. What do you feel you can learn about a person from his or her picture?

Strawberries

· ·

Directions: Discuss the man in this picture with several of your classmates. Try to agree on answers to the questions at the bottom of the page. Write short answers in the blanks, and be prepared to tell the class why you answered as you did.

What nationality do you think this man is? Why? _____

Does he speak English? _____

How old is he? _____

Is he married? Does he have any children? _____

What does he do for a living? _____

Would you like to meet him? Why or why not? _____

Midnight

Directions: Discuss the man in this picture with several classmates. Try to agree on answers to the questions at the bottom of the page. Write short answers in the blanks, and be prepared to tell the class why you answered as you did.

1. What is the man doing? Why do you think so? _____

   _____

2. What do you think has happened? (Circle the letter of your answer.)

   a. His company just announced it was going out of business.
   b. He thinks he has heard a burglar in the house.
   c. He left his car unlocked with the keys in it.
   d. His daughter has not come home yet.
   e. His favorite late night show on television has just been canceled.

3. Actually this picture is from a magazine advertisement. What do you suppose it is advertising? Circle the letter of your answer. Be prepared to explain your choice.

   a. a hotel
   b. sleeping pills
   c. toothpaste
   d. a bank
   e. pajamas

On the Phone

Directions: Discuss the woman in this picture with several classmates. Try to agree on answers to the questions at the bottom of the page. Write short answers in the blanks, and be prepared to tell the class why you answered as you did.

© Corbis

1. What kind of work do you think this woman does? What is her job title?

   _____

2. What kind of emotion is she expressing? What makes you think so?

   _____

3. Who is she speaking to on the phone?

   _____

4. What did the person on the phone just say to her?

   _____

5. What is the woman thinking?

   _____

Work with a partner. Prepare a short telephone dialogue that tells the story behind this picture. Present your dialogue to the rest of the class.

Here's a picture for you to look at. A picture can tell you a lot about a person. What do you feel you can learn about a person from his or her picture?

What's Going On?

Directions: Discuss the man in this picture with several classmates. Try to agree on answers to the questions at the bottom of the page. Write short answers in the blanks, and be prepared to tell the class why you answered as you did.

1. What is this man's nationality? What language does he speak? Why do you think so?

   _____

   _____

2. What is he doing? How does he feel?_____

   _____

   _____

3. What do you think has just happened?_____

   _____

4. What do you think the man is going to say?_____

   _____

5. Using only your hands and the expression on your face, try to show the following emotions so that your classmates can understand:

a. anger	d. fear	g. "You must be joking!"
b. surprise	e. impatience	h. "Believe me, it's not my fault!"
c. doubt	f. joy	i. "Just a minute; not so fast!"

Memory Skills

Did you ever study for an examination and then forget everything you learned? Memory is very important, both on the job and in school. This activity will exercise your memory and help you learn how not to forget.

Summer Day

Directions: Look at the picture for two minutes. Think about the entire scene. Carefully note all the details as your eyes move from left to right. Think about these questions: Where is the scene taking place? What is the weather like? What is happening? Where did the people come from? What do you think will happen next? Now turn your paper over and on another piece of paper, write down as many things as you can that are in the picture. Then answer the questions about the picture. Do not look at the picture again until you have completed your list.

Now try to answer questions without looking back at the picture.

1. Is the airplane flying towards the east (the right) or the west (the left)? _____

2. How many boys are in the water? _____

3. Are the cows all black, spotted, or all white? _____

4. Is the barn door open or closed? _____

5. Are there two or three wires on the barbed wire fence? _____

6. What does the dog have in its mouth? _____

7. What is on the roof of the barn? _____

8. What does the sign on the tree say? _____

Turn back to the picture and check your answers. How good was your memory?

Now try the picture below. This time you will make up questions about the picture. Then ask your partner these questions, and answer your partner's questions.

*Did you ever study for an examination and
then forget everything you learned? Memory is
very important, both on the job and in school.
This activity will exercise your memory and
help you learn how not to forget.*

Lists

• •

Directions: On the back of this page is a list of twenty words. You will have two minutes to
look at the list and memorize the words. Then write as many of these words as possible in
the space below. *You do not have to write them in the same order.* Your teacher will tell you when
to look at the words.

1. _____   11. _____

2. _____   12. _____

3. _____   13. _____

4. _____   14. _____

5. _____   15. _____

6. _____   16. _____

7. _____   17. _____

8. _____   18. _____

9. _____   19. _____

10. _____   20. _____

After you have written all the words you can remember, be prepared to talk with other people in the class about any systems you may have used in memorizing the words and any special problems you may have had in trying to remember them.

Here is the list of twenty words. You have two minutes to memorize them.

1. angry

2. banker

3. bicycle

4. candy

5. chair

6. cow

7. desk

8. fear

9. floor

10. healthy

11. lamp

12. love

13. milk

14. nurse

15. onions

16. peanuts

17. sad

18. student

19. towel

20. wife

Did you ever study for an examination and then forget everything you learned? Memory is very important, both on the job and in school. This activity will exercise your memory and help you learn how not to forget.

The Human Skeleton

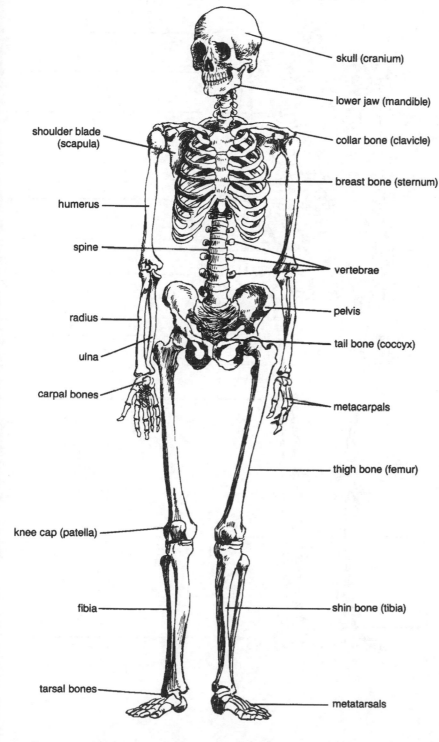

skull (cranium)

lower jaw (mandible)

collar bone (clavicle)

breast bone (sternum)

shoulder blade (scapula)

humerus

spine

radius

ulna

carpal bones

vertebrae

pelvis

tail bone (coccyx)

metacarpals

thigh bone (femur)

knee cap (patella)

fibia

shin bone (tibia)

tarsal bones

metatarsals

Directions:

1. Listen to your teacher pronounce the name of each bone.

2. Repeat the pronunciation after your teacher.

3. Look carefully at the spelling. Copy the word, and at the same time, pronounce it again.

4. After you have heard, spoken, read, and written the name of each bone, review all the names with a partner for several minutes. Quiz each other.

5. Test yourself! Turn this page over and find out how well you have memorized these twenty bones of the human skeleton.

On each line below, write the name of the bone that the line points to. Do not look back at the answers!

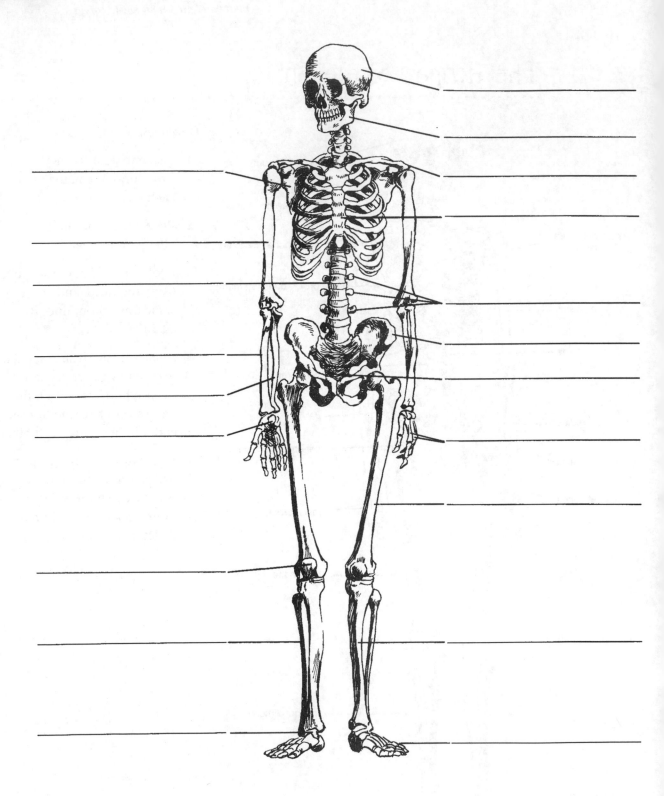

Did you ever study for an examination and then forget everything you learned? Memory is very important, both on the job and in school. This activity will exercise your memory and help you learn how not to forget.

Tool Shop

Directions:

1. Listen to your teacher pronounce the name of each tool. Repeat each word aloud.

2. Work with a partner. Look at each picture. Decide the use of each tool. If you are not sure, ask another student or look up the word in the dictionary.

3. With you partner, study the spelling of each word. Pronounce the word as you write it. Check and correct your spelling.

4. Quiz your partner on the tool names. Cover the word as you point to a picture and ask, "What's this?" "How do you spell . . .?" Let your partner quiz you, too. Important: On the test page, these tools will be shown in a different order. As you learn each name, concentrate on how the tool looks and how it is used. Do not focus on where the picture is on the page.

5. Do not turn the page until your teacher tells you.

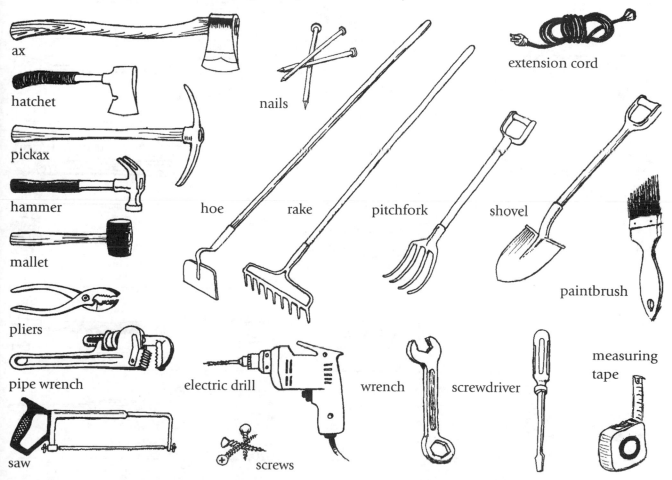

ax

hatchet

pickax

hammer

mallet

pliers

pipe wrench

saw

nails

hoe

rake

screws

electric drill

pitchfork

shovel

wrench

screwdriver

extension cord

paintbrush

measuring tape

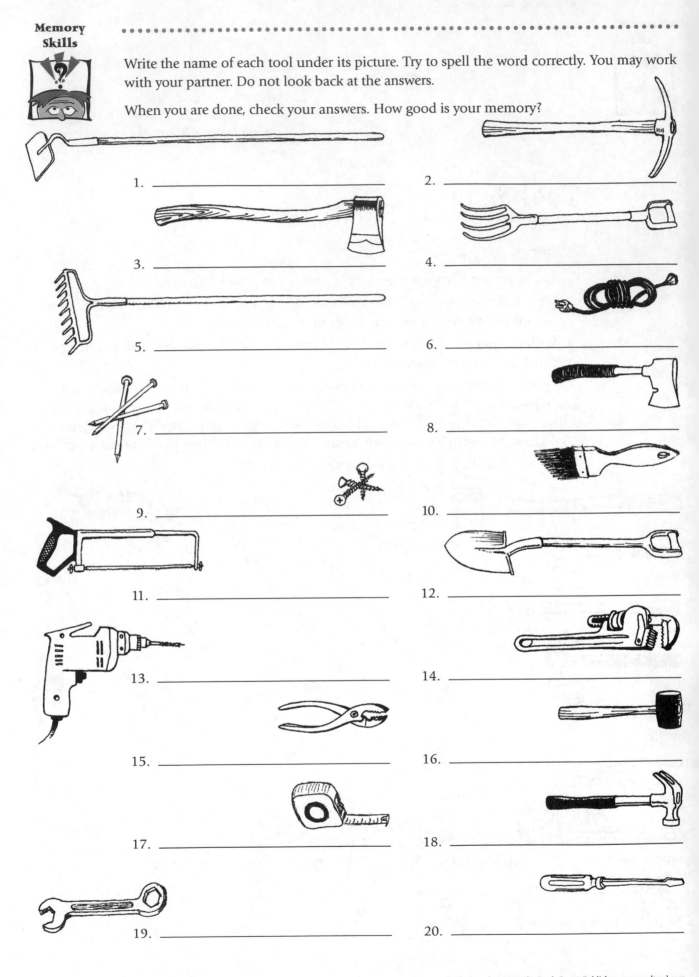

Write the name of each tool under its picture. Try to spell the word correctly. You may work with your partner. Do not look back at the answers.

When you are done, check your answers. How good is your memory?

1. _____

2. _____

3. _____

4. _____

5. _____

6. _____

7. _____

8. _____

9. _____

10. _____

11. _____

12. _____

13. _____

14. _____

15. _____

16. _____

17. _____

18. _____

19. _____

20. _____

Did you ever study for an examination and then forget everything you learned? Memory is very important, both on the job and in school. This activity will exercise your memory and help you learn how not to forget.

The Zodiac

* *

Directions: Study this page with your partner. Try to think of ways to link the name of each zodiac sign with its picture and symbol. Try naming each picture with your partner and memorizing the phrase. For example: "Taurus the bull," "Gemini the twins." Next, try to associate each symbol with its matching picture. For example: the symbol for Leo looks like a lion's tail; the symbol for Capricorn looks like a goat leaping down a mountain slope. Remember, it's much easier to memorize twelve sets than thirty-six unrelated items.

Do not turn the page over until your teacher tells you.

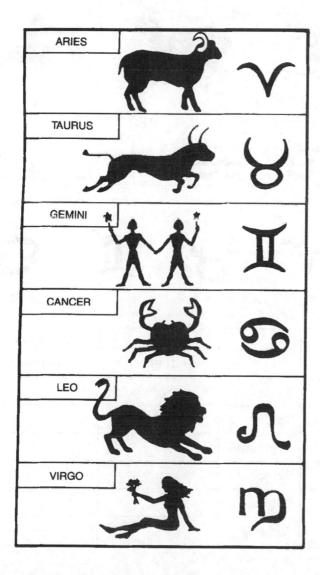

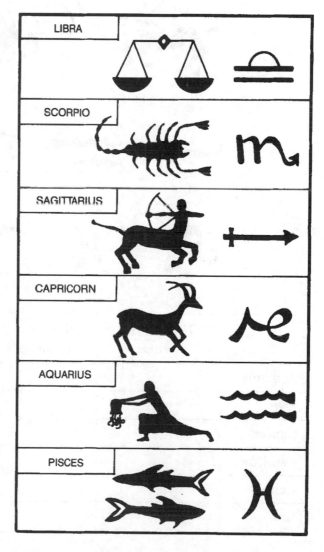

At the bottom of this page is an alphabetical list of the twelve zodiac signs. Use the letters and numbers of the mixed up pictures and symbols. Match the name of each sign with its correct picture and symbol. You may work on this quiz with your partner. Do not turn the page over to the answers.

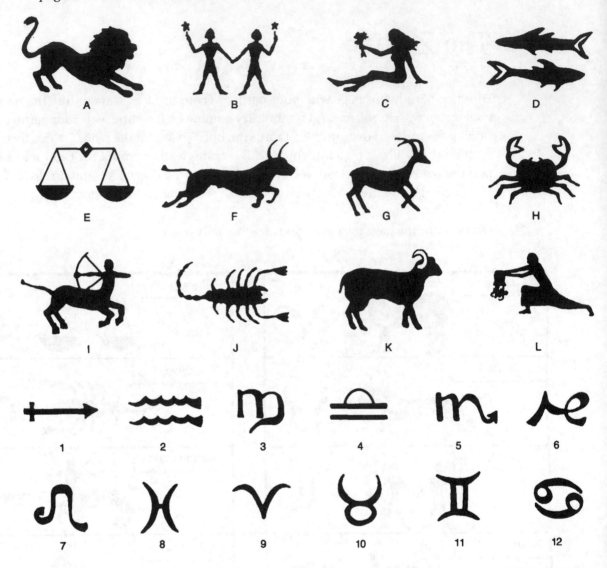

	The Picture Letter	The Symbol Number		The Picture Letter	The Symbol Number
Aquarius			Libra		
Aries			Pisces		
Cancer			Sagittarius		
Capricorn			Scorpio		
Gemini			Taurus		
Leo			Virgo		

Crossword Puzzles

The Calendar

Countries, Nationalities, and Languages

Tag Questions

Irregular Verbs 1

Irregular Verbs 2

Comparisons

Two-Word Verbs

Who Murdered Mrs. Van Tingle?

In a crossword puzzle, you fill the blanks with letters to make words. Some of the words go across, from left to right. Some of them go down, from top to bottom. Where two words cross each other, the same letter is used in each word. Here's a crossword puzzle for you to solve. Be sure that your answers have the right number of letters and that they "interlock" properly with each other.

The Calendar

Directions: Look at the definitions below. Use them to complete the puzzle. Number 1 *across* and number 1 *down* are done for you.

Across

1. This month is the end of spring and the beginning of summer.
6. This month follows 13 *down*.
7. Abbreviation of the day in the middle of the week.
8. This usually has 365 days.
11. A month in spring.
14. A special day, the first day of the new week.
16. Abbreviation of a winter month.
18. The day before 20 *across*.
19. Abbreviation of the month that begins the fall season.
20. The last school day of the week.

Down

1. The first month of the year.
2. Abbreviation of the shortest month of the year.
3. The first full month of spring.
4. A summer month.
5. Saturday and Sunday.
9. The third day of the week.
10. Abbreviation of the first workday of the week.
12. The summer month after 4 *down*.
13. Named for the eighth month, this month is now the tenth.
15. There are seven of these in a week.
17. Abbreviation of the favorite day of students.

Countries, Nationalities, and Languages

Directions: Work with a partner to solve this crossword puzzle. The answers are all either the names of countries, the names of languages, or the names of nationalities. Use a dictionary or encyclopedia if you are unsure of an answer.

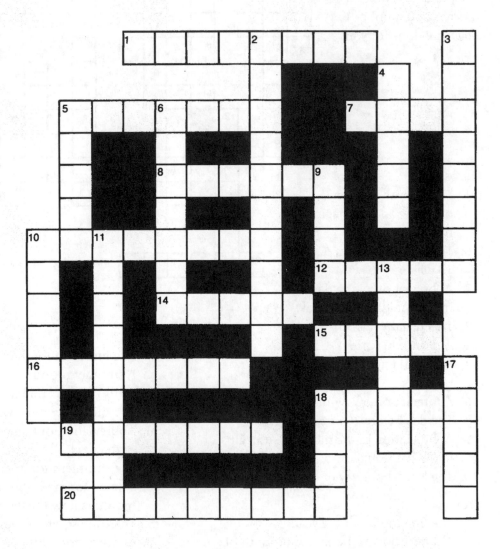

Springboards © 2004 Alta Book Center Publishers • www.altaesl.com
Permission granted to photocopy for one teacher's classroom use only.

Across

1. A citizen of Peru is called this.
5. This is the language spoken in Rome.
7. Farsi is spoken in this country.
8. Portuguese is the official language of this country in South America.
10. This refers to someone or something that comes from Japan.
12. Madrid is the capital of this country in Europe.
14. Katmandu is the capital of this country between Tibet and India.
15. Baghdad on the Tigris River is the capital of this country.
16. Wien is the German name for the capital of this country in Central Europe.
18. Of all the countries in the world, this country has the largest population.
19. Although English is the official language of this West African country, Hausa, Ibo, and Yoruba are the main native languages.
20. Spanish is the language of this South American country.

Down

2. Someone who lives in the capital city called Caracas is called this.
3. This is a citizen of the country whose capital is Ottawa.
4. This is a citizen of Iraq.
5. There are fourteen official languages in this country, the capital of which is Delhi.
6. Beirut is the capital of this Middle Eastern country.
9. Lao is the language spoken in this Southeast Asian country.
10. Arabic is spoken in this Middle Eastern country.
11. This ancient biblical area now includes Israel and Jordan.
13. Over 220 million people speak this language.
17. Tokyo is the capital of this country.
18. Spanish is the language of this island in the Caribbean.

This puzzle focuses on tag questions. A tag question is a short question that follows a statement. It asks you to agree with the statement. Of course, you may not agree. When a person uses a tag question, however, that person expects or hopes that you will agree with the statement. When someone says, "She's a beautiful baby, isn't she?" that person expects that you will agree that the baby is beautiful!

Tag Questions

Directions: Complete the puzzle. Do not use apostrophes. Write *cant,* for example, instead of *can't.* To indicate space between words, write a plus sign (✛). Number 3 *across* is done for you.

Across

3. *Star Wars* was a good movie, _____ _____?

6. If I dropped these eggs on the floor, they'd probably break, _____ _____?

7. Maria hoped that she would be elected Beauty Queen, _____ _____?

9. The children will be happy when school ends, _____ _____?

11. I'm the best student in this class, _____ _____?

14. Betty and I really shouldn't fight with our baby brother, _____ _____?

15. That man isn't your father, _____ _____?

Down

1. I can speak English better than Armando, _____ _____?

2. You don't understand this math problem, _____ _____?

4. Tomorrow should be a sunny day, _____ _____?

5. Miss O'Grady is a very good teacher, _____ _____?

8. We haven't had an English test in weeks, _____ _____?

10. I won't have to stay after school today, _____ _____?

11. I'm not supposed to know about the party, _____ _____?

12. This puzzle isn't difficult, _____ _____?

13. I don't have to get a perfect score, _____ _____?

Irregular Verbs 1

Directions: Work with a partner to complete this puzzle. Think of the right verb for each sentence. Then write it in the puzzle.

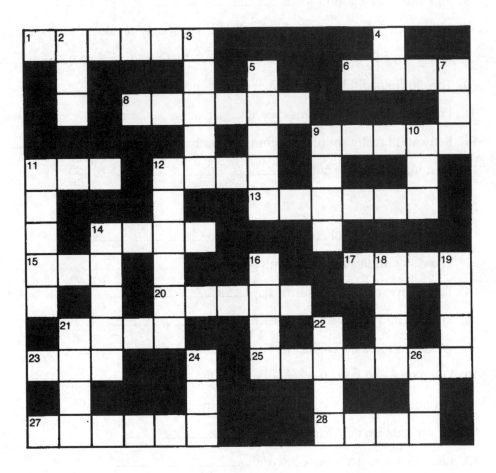

Across

1. You should _____ jelly on your bread with a knife, not a spoon.

6. When the woman slipped on the ice, she _____ and broke her arm.

8. My radio is _____ and doesn't work.

9. Jack's alarm clock didn't work, so he _____ until noon.

11. Yesterday, Hernando _____ himself while shaving.

12. *Gone with the Wind* is the best movie I've ever _____.

13. Our teacher _____ us all these irregular verbs last week.

14. The hunter aimed his rifle and _____ the bear.

15. My roommate _____ at his desk and studied all night.

17. Last year, Agatha's little boy _____ three inches taller.

20. Jack had never _____ pickled pig's feet until last night.

21. Richard has never _____ the same tie two days in a row.

23. Uncle Oscar _____ cat food to his dog by mistake.

25. Ben _____ about the problem for a long time, but he couldn't solve it.

27. The police discovered that a thief had _____ money from the Police Department safe!

28. The baby's crying _____ everyone in the house awake all night.

Down

2. John _____ his hands in his pockets.

3. Martin _____ his car so fast that he got a ticket for speeding.

4. "I'd like to visit you. Will you _____ home around four o'clock?"

5. Fred understood what Maria said, but he wasn't sure what she _____.

7. Martha wouldn't _____ her daughter stay up and watch television.

9. It's cold in here. Please _____ the window.

10. Irene was sure she had _____ a pen in her purse that morning.

11. I wasn't sure which hat to choose, but I finally _____ the red one.

12. Betty and Bob have been angry and haven't _____ to each other for a week.

14. Everyone _____ when the judge entered the room. Then they sat down again.

16. I _____ sorry for Mrs. Bennett when her husband died.

18. The students left the room quietly when the fire alarm bell _____.

19. We wanted to go to Acapulco, but we _____ to Puerto Vajarta instead

21. Ben _____ when his cat died.

22. Ann told Billy not to take any cookies from the jar, but he _____ six.

24. Mrs. Tremble has _____ two miles every day this week.

26. Hank Aaron has _____ more home runs than any other baseball player in history.

Irregular Verbs 2

Directions: Work with a partner to complete this puzzle. Think of the right verb for each sentence. Then write it in the puzzle.

Across

1. John was asked to bring cola to the party, but he _____ ginger ale instead.
8. It was so quiet in the house that you could have _____ a pin drop.
9. It is sad to see that the people have _____ all their garbage into the river.
10. Have I ever _____ you the funny story about my sister-in-law?
11. Someone had _____ a picture of the teacher on the board.
14. The soldiers _____ hard in the battle, but were defeated.
16. The queen remained standing, but the people _____ in front of her.
17. Jenny _____ her car for more than she paid for it.
21. Hector had _____ a letter to his grandmother a week before she died.
22. Tom _____ Elena that she couldn't beat him in a foot race, but he lost.
23. Our school _____ the basketball championship last year.
24. Betty didn't know George, but she _____ his brother Paul.
25. Gerald carefully _____ his signature on the check.
28. Maria's hat was _____ off by the wind.
32. Carlo's a good Boy Scout and has always _____ at least one good deed a day.
33. Last year the cost of living _____ to its highest level in ten years.
34. No one knew where Aunt Florence had secretly _____ her diary.
35. King Henry himself _____ his soldiers into battle at Agincourt.

Down

2. The Lone Ranger _____ a beautiful white horse named Silver.
3. Gloria was pleased when she _____ an A on her English test.
4. Sid _____ stones at the dog and then wondered why it was so friendly.
5. The crowd stood up and _____ the national anthem.
6. The earthquake _____ our building so much that some of the walls cracked.
7. Toshi _____ a boy $5.00 to wash his car for him.
11. The dog _____ a hole in the yard and buried its bone.
12. She _____ in trouble for cheating.
13. It's a well _____ fact that Columbus arrived in America in 1492.
14. When the winter ended, the birds _____ back north again.
15. Little Willie fell and _____ his knee.
17. Reiko dropped her camera in the lake and it _____ to the bottom.
18. The Beatles _____ large crowds wherever they went.
19. My dog barks a lot, but he has never actually _____ anyone.
20. The baseball star _____ at the ball and missed.
22. How long have you _____ studying English?
26. Have you ever _____ on a motorcycle at 100 miles per hour?
27. The party was _____ in an old bar.
29. The teacher _____ a dictionary on my desk and told me to use it.
30. Because it was so cold, Alberto _____ a woolen scarf around his neck.
31. When Jack cut his finger, it _____ for five minutes without stopping!

In a crossword puzzle, you fill the blanks with letters to make words. Some of the words go across, from left to right. Some of them go down, from top to bottom. Where two words cross each other, the same letter is used in each word. Here's a crossword puzzle for you to solve. Be sure that your answers have the right number of letters and that they "interlock" properly with each other.

Two-Word Verbs

Directions: Work with a partner to solve this crossword puzzle. Look at the clues. Read each definition, and then complete the sentence with the correct two-word verb. As you write the two words in the correct spaces of the puzzle, use a plus sign (✛) to indicate the space between the verb and the preposition. Use both the definition and the sentence context to help you guess the appropriate two-word verb. Number 1 *across* is done for you.

• •

Across

1. *(to allow someone or something to enter)*
Please open the door and _____
_____ the cat.

3. *(to remove clothes)* Johnny was wet from
the rain so his mother told him to
_____ _____ his clothes.

5. *(to present a report to someone in author-
ity)* The teacher told her students that
they must _____ _____ their
homework on Friday.

7. *(to cause)* Science has helped to
_____ _____ many changes in
our lives.

11. *(to indicate)* From this group of
pictures, please _____ _____ the
person you think stole your purse.

13. *(to use scissors to make pieces out of something whole)* The children _____
_____ the newspaper into tiny pieces
and then threw them into the air like
snow.

15. *(to reduce something to a useless state)* A
runner's shoes often _____ _____
quickly from so much running.

16. *(to put on clothing to test the fit or appear-
ance)* You should _____ _____ the
coat before you buy it.

17. *(to miss or not take advantage of something)* When you're in Paris, be sure not
to _____ _____ a chance to see the
Eiffel Tower.

18. *(to postpone, to delay)* Because of the
rain, we'll have to _____ _____
the game until tomorrow.

Down

2. *(to find, or to be found)* Keep looking!
Your watch is likely to _____
_____ somewhere.

4. *(to learn, to discover)* Mrs. Jones was
afraid her husband would _____
_____ about the surprise party
for him.

5. *(to distribute)* You must be sure to
_____ _____ only one test
to each student.

6. *(to reject, to refuse)* Ed thought the
offer of a new job was too good to
_____ _____ .

8. *(to meet by chance)* My hometown is
so small that you're likely to _____
_____ family or friends on the main
street.

9. *(to complete a second time)* The teacher
was unhappy with my homework
and asked me to _____ _____
the last part.

10. *(to continue)* Don't give up! If you
don't succeed at first, you must
_____ _____ trying.

12. *(to survive, to continue one's way of life)*
Albert earned just enough money for
his family to _____ _____ .

14. *(to extinguish)* The Fire Department
was able to _____ _____ the fire
before it destroyed our house.

In a crossword puzzle, you fill the blanks with
letters to make words. Some of the words go
across, from left to right. Some of them
go down, from top to bottom. Where two words
cross each other, the same letter is used in each
word. Here's a crossword puzzle for you to
solve. Be sure that your answers have the right
number of letters and that they "interlock"
properly with each other.

Who Murdered Mrs. Van Tingle?

Directions: To solve the puzzle, first read the story. Guess what words fill the blanks. Then see
if the letters will fit in the puzzle. How good of a detective are you? If you complete this crossword puzzle correctly, you will know who murdered Mrs. Van Tingle.

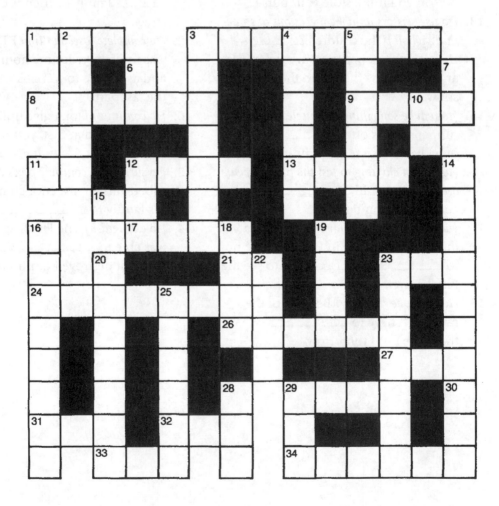

Springboards © 2004 Alta Book Center Publishers • www.altaesl.com
Permission granted to photocopy for one teacher's classroom use only.

Mrs. Van Tingle was dead. There was no question about _____ (11 *across*). The silver letter

opener in her heart and the bloodstain on the carpet left no doubt. The question was who

would want to _____ (18 *down*) her.

    Detective Wiseman stood in the library where the body had been found. He looked

at each of the four persons who were in the house at the time. "All of you," he said,

"_____ (28 *down*) suspects."

    The first suspect was Jonas P. Munnymaker, the family _____ (8 *across*). Two days

before, he had been asked by Mrs. Van Tingle to change her will. At first, he

_____ (25 *down*) with her and urged her not to make any changes, but he finally agreed

to do so. She was killed, however, before she was able to sign the new will.

    The second suspect was Mrs. Van Tingle's younger _____ (4 *down*), Rowena. Her

husband had just left her because of a secret he discovered about her _____ (9 *across*).

Rowena was sure that _____ (15 *across*) had heard the secret from her older sister, who was

always whispering in his _____ (32 *across*). Rowena was _____ (10 *down*) angry that she

went to see her sister immediately. She told the detective, however, that her sister was killed

before she had the chance to discuss the matter with her.

    The third suspect was William Inkster Van Tingle, a _____ (5 *down*) who was known

to his friends as Winky. He had run away from his _____ (3 *down*) and, after a year, he

decided to ask his aunt for money. He had been staying in her house for _____ (27 *across*)

days, but he told Dr. Wiseman he hadn't yet asked her for money.

    The fourth suspect was Dobson, the family butler for _____ (34 *across*) years. He

planned to retire soon and expected _____ (30 *across*) large amount of money from his

employer. Perhaps this was why he was unhappy when he learned that Mrs. Van Tingle

intended to change her will.

    Detective Wiseman reviewed the facts. Mrs. Van Tingle had tea with her sister, nephew,

and lawyer around 4:00. _____ (7 *down*) 5:00, Dobson removed the tea tray and

returned to the kitchen. Rowena went upstairs to her bedroom, saying that she wanted

to read for a while. Jonas Munnymaker went into the living room to smoke his

_____ pipe. (Mrs. Van Tingle disapproved of smoking and would not allow
(16 *down*)

anyone to smoke in her presence.) Winky asked his aunt if he could talk with her alone.

She said that she had some _____ letters she wanted to read in private, but she
(3 *across*)

agreed to meet him _____ the library at 5:30.
(21 *across*)

At about 5:20, according to Dobson, Mrs. Van Tingle _____ for him from
(12 *across*)

the library. She was upset because she could not find her silver letter opener. While looking

for it, they were happy to find a _____ earring, which Mrs. Van Tingle had
(24 *across*)

recently lost. They were also surprised to find Rowena's _____ behind the desk.
(20 *down*)

However, they couldn't find the letter opener anywhere. Because Mrs. Van Tingle had

a large package to open, Dobson went in to the kitchen to get her a knife so she could

_____ the string. On the way, he took Rowena's glasses up to her room, but
(23 *across*)

she wasn't there. When he returned to the library, he was shocked to see Mrs. Van Tingle

lying on the floor beside the _____. The silver letter opener was stuck deep into
(17 *across*)

her _____.
(2 *down*)

Detective Wiseman looked closely at the desk. It was _____ and
(22 *down*)

_____, typical of the personal habits of its owner. Beside an ashtray with a pipe
(19 *down*)

in it, he was surprised to see an open Webster's _____ and a pile of airmail
(14 *down*)

letters, neatly opened. But he did not see the package that Dobson had mentioned.

The detective looked at each of the suspects. The sister's _____ were
(13 *across*)

_____ from crying. The nephew shifted from one foot to the other. The lawyer
(12 *down*)

seemed worried as he _____ on the _____ and adjusted and read-
(29 *down*)   (29 *across*)

justed his _____. The butler stood _____ the door, looking
(31 *across*)   (6 *down*)

_____ and still holding the kitchen knife he had gone to get.
(33 *across*)

After a long silence, the detective finally spoke. "One of you is guilty of murder, and

now I am _____ who it is." He turned and pointed his finger. "I accuse *you!* You
(23 *down*)

are the murderer of Mrs. Van Tingle," he shouted at _____ _____.
(1 *across*)   (26 *across*)

WHO DID HE POINT TO? HOW DID HE KNOW?

In a crossword puzzle, you fill the blanks with letters to make words. Some of the words go across, from left to right. Some of them go down, from top to bottom. Where two words cross each other, the same letter is used in each word. Be sure that your answers have the right number of letters and that they "interlock" properly with each other.

We often describe a thing by comparing it to something else. Many comparisons of this kind are used over and over so that they have become part of the language. This puzzle uses twenty of these common comparisons.

Comparisons

· ·

Directions: Complete the puzzle by writing the adjectives that are used in the following common expressions.

Across

4. as _____ as a ghost
7. as _____ as a mule
9. as _____ as a cucumber
10. as _____ as a fox
12. as _____ as gold
15. as _____ as a post
16. as _____ as A B C
17. as _____ as a rose
18. as _____ as a bee

Down

1. as _____ as a house
2. as _____ as lead
3. as _____ as an ox
4. as _____ as toast
5. as _____ as a peacock
6. as _____ as a mouse
7. as _____ as an eel
8. as _____ as a bat
11. as _____ as a feather
13. as _____ as dirt
14. as _____ as nails

You Be the Judge

Mr. Brown and Mrs. Green

Bus Fare

To Be in Miami

The Case of the Unhappy Worker

To Pass or Not to Pass

When two people can't settle an argument by talking about it, they sometimes go to court. Each person tells his or her side of the argument to a judge. The judge then decides which one is right. This is a real case that was brought before a judge. But now, you will be the judge!

Mr. Brown and Mrs. Green

Directions: Read the following case. Then discuss it. Decide who you think was right, and be ready to tell why you think so. In other words—you be the judge.

Mr. and Mrs. Brown were divorced after ten years of marriage and two children, Billy and Betty. A year after their divorce, Mrs. Brown remarried. She became Mrs. Green. However, Mr. Brown, as her first husband, refused to allow his children to be called by the second husband's name. They were his children, he told the judge, and their names should remain Billy and Betty Brown.

His former wife did not agree. "The difference in their last name and my married name would confuse people. It would embarrass the children," she argued. "They would feel insecure. Furthermore, why shouldn't they have my second husband's name? Now he supports them, and their own father doesn't."

"Your Honor," Mr. Brown told the judge, "my wife's real reason for wanting this change is to hide the failure of her first marriage. She wants our children to be called Billy and Betty Green for her own convenience, not for the sake of the children who love me and call me daddy."

You Be the Judge: Would you allow the family name of the children to be changed?

After you have discussed this case, write your decision and the reasons for it.

_____

_____

_____

_____

_____

_____

_____

_____

_____

_____

Bus Fare

Directions: Read the following case. Then discuss it. Decide who you think was right, and be ready to tell why you think so. In other words—you be the judge.

When Mrs. Rider got on the bus and paid her fare with a five-dollar bill, the driver became angry. He refused her money. He shouted that he wasn't required to change anything larger than a dollar.

"But I have nothing smaller," Mrs. Rider pleaded. "And I'm already late for work."

"I can't help that, lady!" the bus driver yelled. "You can't ride for nothing, so you'll have to get off."

Mrs. Rider sued the bus company. "I lost my job because I arrived late to work," she told the judge. "Also, the bus driver was rude. He embarrassed and upset me in public. Certainly he could have changed a five-dollar bill if he wished."

The company lawyer argued, "We are a bus company, not a bank. We are always willing to change reasonable amounts. But the driver has neither the time nor the cash to change large bills."

You Be the Judge: Would you decide for the bus company or for Mrs. Rider?

After you have discussed this case, write your decision and the reasons for it.

_____

_____

_____

_____

_____

_____

_____

_____

_____

When two people can't settle an argument by talking about it, they sometimes go to court. Each person tells his or her side of the argument to a judge. The judge then decides which one is right. This is a real case that was brought before a judge. But now, you will be the judge!

To Be in Miami

Directions: Read the following case. Then discuss it. Decide who you think was right, and be ready to tell why you think so. In other words—you be the judge.

Max was the owner of a fancy hotel on a favorite Miami Beach site. At first he was not worried when the owner of the hotel next door announced that he was going to make his hotel taller. Then Max realized with horror that this change would block the sun from his beach. Worried that his hotel business would be destroyed, Max rushed into court.

"Don't let them block the sun from my hotel, judge." Max cried. "My guests expect to be in sunshine all day. The law requires a person to use his property so it doesn't interfere with the rights of others. If the neighboring hotel is made taller, it should not cut the afternoon sun off my beach."

"We're entitled to build whatever we please on our own property," a representative for the other hotel replied, "as long as it doesn't interfere with Max's legal rights. As for sunshine, Max doesn't own the sun."

You Be the Judge: Would you decide for Max or the other hotel owner?

After you have discussed this case, write your decision and the reasons for it.

_____

_____

_____

_____

_____

_____

_____

_____

_____

_____

When two people can't settle an argument by talking about it, they sometimes go to court. Each person tells his or her side of the argument to a judge. The judge then decides which one is right. This is a real case that brought before a judge. But now, you will be the judge!

The Case of the Unhappy Worker

Directions: Read the following case. Then discuss it. Decide who you think was right, and be ready to tell why you think so. In other words—you be the judge.

John was very unhappy in his job. As a result, he decided to give his boss two months' notice. At the end of the two months, he would leave the company.

When John told his boss he was planning to resign in two months, the boss became very angry. He told John to leave the company at once. John thought this meant that he was fired.

When people were fired in that company, they were given severance pay. Therefore, John demanded his severance pay of more than $2000. John's boss refused, so John sued him in court.

"My resignation did not take effect for two months," John told the judge. "I wasn't ready to leave immediately, but he told me to get out. That is the same as firing me, and therefore I deserve severance pay."

"John ended his employment voluntarily," the boss argued. "I simply accelerated the process for him. Why should he mind that?"

You Be the Judge: Would you award John severance pay?

After you have discussed this case, write your decision and the reasons for it.

_____

_____

_____

_____

_____

_____

_____

_____

_____

_____

_____

When two people can't settle an argument by talking about it, they sometimes go to court. Each person tells his or her side of the argument to a judge. The judge then decides which one is right. This is a real case that was brought before a judge. But now, you will be the judge!

To Pass or Not to Pass

Directions: Read the following case. Then discuss it. Decide who you think was right, and be ready to tell why you think so. In other words—you be the judge.

Hortense Smith was driving behind a huge truck on a narrow, winding country road. Because she could not see ahead of the truck, she was afraid to pass it. The truck driver, looking in his mirror, noticed her difficulty. He signed with his hand that it was safe for her to pass.

Unfortunately, the truck driver misjudged the speed of an oncoming car. It crashed into Mrs. Smith's car and seriously injured her. She sued the truck company for damages.

"I relied on the driver's signal that it was safe to pass," she told the judge. "Because he was wrong to signal me to go ahead, he should pay for my accident that he caused."

"You should not have relied on our driver to tell you how to drive your car," argued the lawyer for the truck company. "After all, you yourself are responsible for your own safety."

You Be the Judge: Would you award damages to Mrs. Smith?

After you have discussed this case, write your decision and the reasons for it.

_____

_____

_____

_____

_____

_____

_____

_____

_____

_____

_____

_____

It's Only Logical

In a "logic puzzle," you use clues from a story to fill in a grid that then helps you answer questions about the story.

Halloween Party

Directions: Read the following story and fill in the grid below it to find the answers.

Halloween is the evening of October 31st, when children play tricks while wearing strange clothes and false faces or masks. Their costumes may look like the clothes of a sailor or cowboy, a queen or a clown. Or they may dress up to look like an animal such as a monkey. Each child puts on a mask so that no one can know who he or she is.

Last year the three sons of Mr. and Mrs. Cooper attended a Halloween party. It was at the home of David, a friend of the Cooper boys. When Mr. Cooper went there to take his sons home, he was unable to recognize him. Everyone was dressed in costumes. Four children stood in front of him. One was dressed as Superman, one was a robot, one was Mickey Mouse, and the fourth was a ghost. Mr. Cooper was sure that the children were his three sons, Arthur, Billy, and Charles, and the host of the party, David. But he could not decide which was which.

	Superman	Robot	Micky Mouse	Ghost
Arthur			O	
Billy			O	
Charles			O	
David	O	O	+	O

Look at the clues below, and help Mr. Cooper decide which costume each boy is wearing. Write + in the grid for *yes* and O for *no*. The first clue is done for you.

1. Mr. Cooper's wife had bought the costumes for their sons. He did not know exactly what costumes she had bought, but he knew she had not bought an animal costume.

2. Mr. Cooper was sure Arthur, the oldest boy, was too tall to be dressed as the robot or the ghost.

3. He was sure that the robot was not Charles.

What costumes were the boys wearing? Use the completed grid to find and explain your answers.

Arthur: _____

Billy: _____

Charles: _____

David: _____

In a "logic puzzle," you use clues from a story to fill in a grid that then helps you answer questions about the story.

The Library Fire

Directions: Read the following story and fill in the grid below it to find the answers.

When the town library burned down, the Fire Chief was sure that it was the result of arson. The Police Chief did not want to believe that anyone would purposely start a fire in the library. However, he agreed to help the Fire Chief to investigate the possibility of arson.

Two police officers also helped: Officer Grey and Officer Black. These four persons carefully searched through the burned ruins of the library looking for evidence of arson.

Each person found one clue: (1) an empty gasoline can, (2) a box of matches, (3) a piece of cloth still wet with oil and only partially burned, and (4) a piece of rubber hose that smelled of gasoline.

	Gasoline Can	Box of Matches	Piece of Cloth	Rubber Hose
Fire Chief				
Police Chief				
Officer Grey				
Officer Black				

Use the following information and the grid in order to decide which person found each of the clues. Write ✓ in the grid for *yes* and *O* for *no*.

1. Officer Black and the Fire Chief did not find the piece of cloth or the rubber hose.

2. At the time the gasoline can was discovered by someone else, the Fire Chief was searching in the basement of the library.

3. The person who found the piece of cloth immediately ran to the Police Chief to tell him about it.

What clue did each person find? Use the completed grid to find and explain your answers.

Fire Chief: _____

Police Chief: _____

Officer Grey: _____

Officer Black: _____

In a "logic puzzle," you use clues from a story to fill in a grid that then helps you answer questions about the story.

The Van Astorbilt Jewels

●●

Directions: Read the following story and fill in the grid below it to find the answers.

The wealthiest woman in Middletown was Mrs. Van Astorbilt. She had the good fortune to marry four times and the sense to see that each husband was richer than the one before. But wealth invites burglary. When her home was robbed, four especially expensive pieces of jewelry were stolen from the safe: (1) a pearl necklace, (2) a gold bracelet, (3) a pair of ruby earrings, and (4) a ring with a large emerald. For the police report, the detective had to know who had given her each piece of jewelry. But Mrs. Van Astorbilt was confused and uncertain. She was sure only that a different husband had given her each of the four pieces.

"I can't really remember who gave me what," she told the detective. "Let me see. I'm sure that Jonathan—he was my fourth husband—Jonathan didn't give me the emerald ring. I'm sure of that. Nor the pearl necklace. Jonathan thought pearls were entirely too common!

"And Cyrus—dear Cyrus, he was my first husband. I just don't remember which piece of jewelry he gave me, but I'm sure it wasn't the ruby earrings. He had much better taste. And it wasn't the emerald ring, because he had already given me a lovely diamond ring as a wedding present.

"Now let me see, there's also the pearl necklace. Who did give it to me? I'm fairly sure it wasn't Cyrus. And I'm positive it wasn't Waldo—Waldo was my dear second husband, a self-made millionaire, but not nearly so wealthy as Sylvester.

"And now, you simply must excuse me," Mrs. Van Astorbilt concluded. "I seem to be very confused about these unimportant details. I'm sorry, I really am. But perhaps you can figure out who gave me what from what I remember my husbands *didn't* give me."

	Pearl Necklace	Gold Bracelet	Ruby Earrings	Emerald Ring
Cyprus				
Waldo				
Sylvester				
Jonathan				

Can you help the detective decide which husband gave which piece of jewelry to Mrs. Van Astorbilt? Use the grid and write ✚ for *yes* and *O* for *no*.

Use the completed grid to find and explain your answers to the questions below.

Who gave Mrs. Van Astorbilt:

the pearl necklace? _____

the gold bracelet? _____

the ruby earrings? _____

the emerald ring? _____

In a

52

A Busy Schedule

Directions: Read the following story and fill in the grid below it to find the answers.

Maria Gomez leads a very active life. She has a busy schedule. As a result, she has to plan her time carefully. Next week she will be especially busy because her mother and father will be visiting her.

Maria works in an office from 9:00 to 5:00 every day. In addition, she has three things she must do every week: (1) clean the house, (2) wash the clothes, and (3) work at the Child Care Center as a volunteer. Furthermore, next week she has promised to (4) go shopping with her mother and (5) take both her parents to visit some old friends. She has time to do only one of these things each day

	Clean the House	Wash the Clothes	Work at the Child Care Center	Go Shopping with Her Mother	Take Her Parents Visiting
Monday					
Tuesday					
Wednesday					
Thursday					
Friday					

Use the following information and the grid to find out what Maria will do each day of next week. Write ✚ in the grid for *yes* and *O* for *no*.

1. Maria will not wash the clothes or take her parents visiting on the first or last day of the week.

2. She will clean the house on a day in the week later than the day when she goes shopping with her mother, but before the day when she works at the Child Care Center or when she washes the clothes.

3. She will not take her parents visiting on Thursday, but she will take them later in the week than the day when she cleans the house.

Use the completed grid to find and explain your answers to the questions below.

What will Maria do on Monday? _____

What will she do on Tuesday? _____

What will she do on Wednesday? _____

What will she do on Thursday? _____

What will she do on Friday? _____

Making the Grade

Directions: Read the following story and fill in the grid below it to find the answers.

Five of Mr. Jordan's students were worried about their final grade in English. They kept asking him what there grades were. Mr. Jordan understood why they were concerned, but the regulations of the school did not allow him to tell students their grades until they were reported to the Student Records Office.

When the five girls kept asking for their grades, he suggested a game. "Listen," he said, "I can't *tell* you your grades, but no regulation says you're not allowed to try to figure them out. I'll give you five clues. From them, each of you should be able to figure out your own grade. Okay?"

The girls agreed enthusiastically.

	A	B	C	D	F
Bertha					
Celeste					
Esther					
Maria					
Pauline					

Using Mr. Jordan's clues, try to determine each girl's grade. Use the following information and the grid. Write ✝ in the grid for *yes* and *O* for *no*.

1. "Well," he said, "there are five different grades: A, B, C, D, and unfortunately F. Each of you has a different grade.

2. "Bertha, you didn't get a C."

3. "Celeste, your grade is lower than Esther's but higher than Pauline's."

4. "Maria, neither you nor Bertha got an A, but one of you, I'm sorry to say, got an F."

5. "Pauline, your grade is lower than Bertha's but higher than Maria's."

Use the completed grid to find and explain your answers to the questions below.

What was Bertha's grade? _____

What was Celeste's grade? _____

What was Esther's grade? _____

What was Maria's grade? _____

What was Pauline's grade? _____

Story Pictures

*See the activity, "Betty Lou," for directions for
using this picture.*

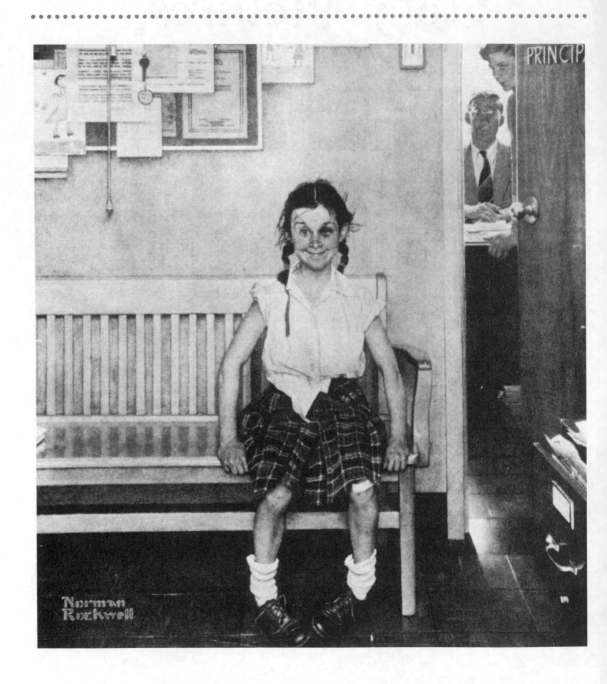

Look at the copy of the painting by Norman Rockwell, an American artist who lived from 1894 to 1978. The painting is of a sixth-grade girl we will call Betty Lou. Betty Lou is in the principal's office at her school. Does the painting tell a story?

Betty Lou

Directions: Look at the painting and use it to help you do this page. You can look back at the picture as often as you like. Your teacher will tell you which activities to do.

A. With a partner or in a small group, talk about the following questions. Your teacher may ask you to write your answers or to report them to the class.

1. Why do you think Betty Lou has been called in to the principal's office?

2. Do you think she often fights with boys in her class?

3. Look at Betty Lou's clothes, her hair, and her face. What do they tell you about what has just happened?

4. A boy stepped on Betty Lou's toes and pulled her pigtails. What did he expect her to do?

5. What did she do instead?

6. Why is Betty Lou smiling?

7. Look at the principal. What can you tell about the way he looks?

8. How do you think the boy looks?

9. Is he likely to get into another fight with Betty Lou? Why or why not?

B. Choose one of the following topics and write a short composition.

1. *Betty Lou's Fight*. Write a story in two paragraphs. In the first paragraph, describe the cause of the fight between Betty Lou and the boy. In the second paragraph, describe the fight and explain why she is now waiting outside the principal's office.

2. *Betty Lou's Interview with the Principal*. Decide how the principal handles the situation. What does he decide to do and what is Betty Lou's reaction?

C. Choose one of the following topics and either hold a debate on it with one person (or one team) arguing in favor of the statement and the other arguing against it, or write about it. If you write, you may argue for it or against it. In either case, whether you debate the topic or write about it, be sure to present a carefully reasoned argument. Support what you say (or write) with strong, carefully thought-out reasons.

1. All women and girls should learn self-defense so they can protect themselves.

2. Schools should encourage a spirit of competition among students.

See the activity, "The Boy on the Chair," for
directions for using this picture.

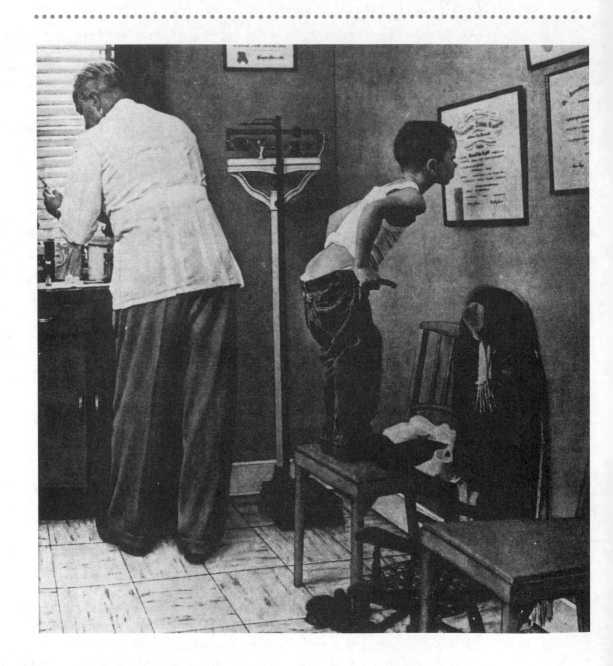

*Look at the copy of the painting by Norman
Rockwell, an American artist who lived from
1894 to 1978. The painting is of a doctor's
office. A young boy is visiting the doctor. Does
the painting tell a story?*

The Boy on the Chair

Directions: Look at the painting and use it to help you do this page. You can look back at the picture as often as you like. Your teacher will tell you which activities to do.

A. With a partner or in a small group, talk about the following questions. Your teacher may ask you to write your answers or to report them to the class.

1. Where is this scene taking place? How do you know?

2. Why do you think the boy is there at this time?

3. Why is the boy partly undressed? What is going to happen?

4. Who is the other person in the picture? How do you know?

5. What is this person doing?

6. Do you think the boy is looking forward to what will happen next? Why or why not?

7. What are the things hanging on the wall?

8. What is the boy doing while he is standing on the chair?

9. Why do you think he is doing this?

10. What season of the year is it? How do you know?

B. Choose one of the following topics and write a short composition.

1. *What and Where.* Write a description in one paragraph of the place shown in the picture. Include as many details as you can. In another paragraph tell what each of the two people in the picture is doing.

2. *"Let Me Tell You . . ."* Write, in the first person, with quotation marks, what the little boy is thinking.

C. Choose one the following topics and either write a short composition about it or give a talk about it. Be ready to answer questions from the class about your topic.

1. Describe how modern medicine in your country has controlled the increase or spread of a serious disease.

2. Should doctors always tell their patients the truth? Some doctors warn patients, "This may hurt a little." Others do not. If you had a serious disease that might be fatal, would you want your doctor to tell you? Is honesty always the best policy in such matters? Why or why not?

*See the activity, "The Babysitter," for directions
for using this picture.*

Look at the copy of the painting by Norman Rockwell, an American artist who lived from 1894 to 1978. The painting is of a babysitter. A babysitter is a person, usually a responsible teenager, who takes care of babies or young children while their parents are out for the evening. Does the painting tell a story?

The Babysitter

Directions: Look at the painting and use it to help you do this page. You can look back at the picture as often as you like. Your teacher will tell you which activities to do.

A. With a partner or in a small group, talk about the following questions. Your teacher may ask you to write your answers or to report them to the class.

   1. How old do you think the baby is? The babysitter?

   2. How long do you think the baby has been crying?

   3. How many kinds of books are in the picture? What are they?

   4. How many kinds of bottles are in the picture? What are they?

   5. How do you think the babysitter has tried to quiet the baby? How can you tell?

   6. Do you think the babysitter will be able to finish her homework? Why or why not?

   7. What do you suppose the parents will say when they return?

   8. What is the babysitter doing now? Why is she doing it?

B. Choose one of the following activities.

   1. *What's Going On?* Either orally or in writing, describe this picture in detail so that a friend can visualize the scene. Describe what the babysitter is doing and why. Describe what the baby is doing.

   2. *It Happened to Me, Too.* Have you had an experience in which everything seemed to go wrong? Either orally or in writing, describe the situation and explained what happened.

C. Assume you are the parent of a one-year-old child. You have to go out for the evening and you need a babysitter. Consider the qualifications—the kind of personality, attitude, and personal habits—you will require in anyone who will take care of your child. In either a composition or an oral presentation to the class, discuss these qualifications and tell why you think they are important.

See the activity, "Looking In, Looking Out,"
for directions for using this picture.

Look at the copy of the painting by Norman Rockwell, an American artist who lived from 1894 to 1978. The painting is of a man washing windows and a woman looking through the window at him. Does the painting tell a story?

Looking In, Looking Out

Directions: Look at the painting and use it to help you do this page. You can look back at the picture as often as you like. Your teacher will tell you which activities to do.

A. With a partner or in a small group, talk about the following questions. Your teacher may ask you to write your answers or to report them to the class.

   1. What work is the man outside the window doing?

   2. What is he standing on?

   3. How else is he supported?

   4. How high up is he? How can you tell?

   5. What is happening inside the office?

   6. What kind of work does the man behind the desk do?

   7. What kind of work does the woman do?

   8. How is the woman feeling? Why is she feeling that way?

   9. The man outside the window just winked at the woman. What do you think she will do next? Why?

B. Choose one of the following topics and write a short composition.

   1. *The Man Outside.* Pretend you are the man outside the window. Describe your job. Tell about the tools you use and how you do the work. Discuss the advantages and disadvantages of your job. Are you happy with your work, or would you rather have a job in an office?

   2. *The Woman.* What do you think the woman is daydreaming about as she looks out the window? Pretend you are the woman. Write her thoughts.

C. Choose one of the following topics and either write a short composition about it or give a talk about it. Be ready to answer questions that your classmates may ask.

   1. Describe the way you think an employer and an employee should behave toward each other. Compare these ideas with the relationship between the employer and an employee in your country.

   2. Different people have different opinions about the most important things in life and the ideal lifestyle. Describe your version of the "good life," the life you'd like to lead. If you wish, tell how it differs from your parents' ideal.

See the activity, "The Verdict," for directions
for using this picture.

Look at the copy of the painting by Norman Rockwell, an American artist who lived from 1894 to 1978. The painting is of a jury. A jury is a group of twelve persons chosen to decide questions of fact in a court of law. In many parts of the United States, the law states that a jury's verdict, or decision of whether someone is guilty or innocent, must be unanimous (all jurors must agree). If the jurors cannot agree on a verdict, the case is tried again, in front of a new jury. Does the painting tell a story?

The Verdict

. . . .

Directions: Look at the painting and use it to help you do this page. You can look back at the picture as often as you like. Your teacher will tell you which activities to do.

A. With a partner or a small group, talk about the following questions. Your teacher may ask you to write your answers or to discuss them with the class.

  1. How many people are in this picture? How many men? How many women?

  2. What does the sign on the door say?

  3. Why are these people in this room?

  4. How long do you think they've been in this room? Why do you think that?

  5. Why are there so many pencils and so much paper on the floor?

  6. What are the ten men doing gathered around the woman?

  7. Do you think the woman believes the accused person is guilty or innocent? Why do you think that?

  8. What do you think the court case is about?

  9. How do you think the men feel about the woman juror?

  10. Do you think the woman will continue to hold her own opinion, or do you think the other jurors will finally persuade her to change her mind? Why do you think so?

B. Choose one of the following topics and either write a short composition or give an oral report to your class.

  1. The man bending over the table with his arm stretched out towards the woman is obviously arguing with her. Make up the facts of the court case being tried, then present the argument in the way this man would.

2. Much of the interest in this picture comes from the fact that it's eleven men against one woman. Who do you feel most sympathetic to in this scene? Why? How would the picture story change if it were eleven women jurors against one man? Would the picture seem more serious or more humorous? Who would you feel the most sympathetic to in the new picture? Why?

C. Choose one of the following topics. Either hold a debate about it, or write a short composition, stating and supporting your opinion.

1. Do you agree or disagree with this statement? The jury system is the best and fairest way to find out what really happened, who is telling the truth, and whether a person is guilty or innocent.

2. It has been said that men think with their heads but women tend to think with their hearts. Do you agree or disagree with this statement? Should there be an even distribution of men and women (six men and six women) on every jury? Why or why not?

Springboards © 2004 Alta Book Center Publishers • www.altaesl.com
Permission granted to photocopy for one teacher's classroom use only.

Classes and Categories

Words

Straw

Stamp

Grouping things into classes or categories is a
convenient way to organize them. This page
will help you think about categories and will
help you learn the names of many things that
belong in these categories.

Words

Directions: Look at the grid below. Notice the category names at the left of each row: colors,
animals, states, etc. There is one letter over each column. Your job is to think of as many words
as you can that begin with that letter and belong to each of the categories. Work with a partner or a team. Your team will get one point for each appropriate word you write on the grid.
You will get one extra point for each word you have that is in no other team's grid. Work fast!
There is a time limit.

	W	O	R	D	S
Colors					
Animals					
States					
Cities					
Fruits and Vegetables					

Grouping things into classes or categories is a convenient way to organize them. This page will help you think about categories and will help you learn the names of many things that belong in these categories.

Straw

Directions: Look at the grid below. Notice the category names at the left of each row: things on a farm, things on a beach, etc. There is one letter over each column. Your job is to think of as many words as you can that begin with that letter and belong to each of the categories. Work with a partner or a team. Your team will get one point for each appropriate word you write on the grid. You will get one extra point for each word you have that is in no other team's grid. Work fast! There is a time limit.

	S	T	R	A	W
Things on a Farm					
Things on a Beach					
Things in a House					
Things in a School					
Things in an Office					

Stamp

Directions: Look at the grid below. With your class, agree upon five categories and write each
category in the first box of each row. Examples: clothes, machines, things that are sweet, etc.
There is one letter over each column. Your job is to think of as many words as you can that
begin with that letter and belong to each of the categories. Work with a partner or a team. Your
team will get one point for each appropriate word you write on the grid. You will get one extra
point for each word you have that is in no other team's grid. Work fast! There is a time limit.

	S	T	A	M	P

Note: You can play this category game on your own. Just draw a grid like the one above and
write five letters across the top (the letters don't have to form a word.) With the other play-
ers, agree on five categories. Write the categories on the left side of the grid. Then set a timer
for five minutes, and play the game!

Using the Telephone

Long Distance

The White Pages

The Yellow Pages

Community Services Numbers

*This activity will give you some practice in
using your telephone directory.*

Long Distance

· ·

Directions: Study the Long Distance Calling material from the telephone directory. Be sure
you understand how to figure telephone rates from Burlington, Vermont, at different times
of the day. Also notice the time zones and the differences in time. Then, with a partner, ask
and answer the following questions.

Note: The charges given on the information chart were true for Burlington, Vermont, when
this book was written, but they may have changed since that time. Use your own telephone
directory for the activity below if possible (otherwise use the information provided).

1. You are in Burlington, Vermont. How much does it cost on a weekday to dial your friend
   in Miami directly and talk for three minutes at the following times?

   a. 11:00 A.M. _____   b. midnight _____   c. 6:00 P.M. _____

2. How much money can you save if you telephone from Burlington to Boston at 9:00 on

   a Tuesday evening instead of 9:00 that morning, and talk for five minutes? _____

3. What are the area codes for these states?

   a. Wyoming _____   b. New Mexico _____   c. Maine _____

4. You want to telephone a friend in these cities. What is the area code?

   a. San Francisco, California _____

   b. Spokane, Washington _____

   c. San Antonio, Texas _____

5. You have to telephone someone in Ottawa, the capital of Canada.

   What is the area code? _____

6. If it is 8:00 A.M. in Washington, D.C.; what time is it in these cities?

   a. Boston, Massachusetts _____

   b. Phoenix, Arizona _____

   c. Dallas, Texas _____

7. You are in Burlington, Vermont. It's Sunday noon. Is it cheaper to telephone Seattle, Washington, and talk for six minutes or to telephone Washington, D.C., and talk for seven minutes? What is the difference?

   _____

8. Make up questions similar to those above, and ask your partner to answer them. You may
   wish to trade questions with other members of the class as well.

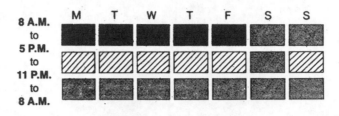

Area Codes and Time Zones

	Dial-direct	Weekday full rate		Evening 40% discount		Night & Weekend 60% discount	
	Mileage Bands						
Sample rates from city of Burlington, VT to:	Airline Miles	First minute	Each additional minute	First minute	Each additional minute	First minute	Each additional minute
Plattsburg, NY	11- 22	.40	.22	.24	.14	.16	.09
Concord, NH	56- 124	.57	.37	.34	.23	.22	.15
Glens Falls, NY	56- 124	.57	.37	.34	.23	.22	.15
Boston, MA	125- 292	.58	.39	.34	.24	.23	.16
Portland, ME	125- 292	.58	.39	.34	.24	.23	.16
Providence, RI	125- 292	.58	.39	.34	.24	.23	.16
Philadelphia, PA	293- 430	.59	.42	.35	.26	.23	.17
Washington, DC	431- 925	.62	.43	.37	.26	.24	.18
Denver, CO	926-1910	.64	.44	.38	.27	.25	.18
Miami, FL	926-1910	.64	.44	.38	.27	.25	.18
Los Angeles, CA	1911-3000	.74	.49	.44	.30	.29	.20
Seattle, WA	1911-3000	.74	.49	.44	.30	.29	.20

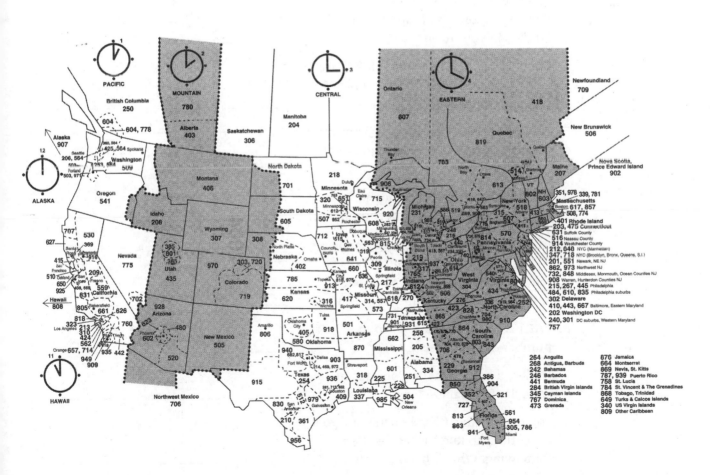

The white pages in a telephone directory list residential information. They give the names, addresses, and telephone numbers of people living in the area. Here's some practice in using the white pages of your telephone directory.

The White Pages

. . . .

Directions: Use the telephone directory white page listings to answer these questions. Notice that the names of towns are abbreviated. A key to the abbreviations is on the following page.

1. You want to go to the Casa Romano Restaurant, but you don't know the address. What is it? _____

2. You have to send a package to New York. What Central Bus Lines number should you call? _____

3. You live in Cameron and want to take dancing lessons. Is Carousel Dance Studios in your town? _____

4. On a cold winter Sunday, your furnace stops working. What is the number of BTU Energy Resources? _____

5. You think a short vacation in Bermuda would be nice. What is the number of Air Travel Tours? _____

6. What is the address and telephone number of Accent Travel in Huntington? _____

7. At a party, you met a married couple with the last name of Austin. You remembered her name is Meg, but you can't recall his name. What is it? _____

8. What is the address and telephone number of BJ's Variety Store? _____

9. Is there a branch of the Continental State Bank in Samoset? _____

10. You recently met Cheryl Adams and you are curious to know what she does for a living. What is her occupation? _____

Now make up questions of your own to ask a partner or the class. Use your own telephone directory white pages if possible. Otherwise use the listings provided. Write your questions below.

_____

_____

_____

_____

_____

_____

Town Abbreviations and Exchange Numbers

Cmrn = Cameron	287	Hunt = Huntington	256	Samo = Samoset	345
EndJ = Enders Junction	372	Jtown = Jamestown	333	Wyby = Waybury	244
		Mlvl = Millville	382		

ABC Day Care Center Circle Dr Samo 345-3928
A-1 Plumbing Svc 24 Main St Mlvl 382-9928
A&R Food Store Main Mall Wyby 244-8059
Abdunur Samir 354 Jefferson Hunt 256-1928
Able A B electrn 12 Smith St Mlvl 382-9928
Able Constance 89 Prospect St EndJ 372-9200
Able Hardware 222 East St Jtown 333-8883
Able Harry dent 10 Main St Wyby 244-8874
Abrusco Ken & Rose 11 Park Pl Samo 345-6628
ACCENT TRAVEL INC
   1182 Charter Rd Cmrn 287-2000
   95 Railroad Av Hunt 256-8217
   Pathways Bus Station Jtown 333-4404
Acheson Chas atty 240 Bank Ln Hunt 256-9928
ACME Paint and Glass Circle Dr Samo 345-9382
Adams Cheryl atty 10 Taft Blvd Hunt 256-1827
Adams E W Culver Ter Hunt 256-2716
Adams Edw & Janet 1 Cindy Pk Wyby 244-1627
Adams Geo phys 2717 Main Jtown 333-4746
Adams Jas D & Barbara A
   26 Greenwood Av EndJ 372-7761
Adams Jas T III 75 Park Pl Mlvl 382-1423
Adams Jos 334 Hapsburg Ct Jtown 333-4646
Adams Rubi & Nancy 14 Oak Ln Samo . . .345-7288
Adamske Eva 949 Pearl St Cmrn 287-7651
Adler Andrew CPA 78 Grant Rd Mlvl 382-1827
ADULT BASIC EDUCATION CENTER
   110 E Spring Rd Wyby 244-3382
   Derringer Dr EndJ 372-4211
   19280 Main St Jtown 333-2271
ADVENTURE TRAVEL 90 Park Rd Samo 345-3450
Ahearn H M 550 Westover Pk Wyby 244-3328
Aimi Celeste 67 North Av Hunt 256-3387
Aimi Thos 100 Courtney Pl Samo 345-9821
AIR TRAVEL TOURS
   Reservations & Information
     Toll Free—Dial '1' & Then 800-936-3837
Airport Gas Airport Plaza Jtown 333-4772
Airport Parking
   Municipal Airport Jtown 333-2727
   Metropolitan Ofc Boston 800-888-4404
Atwater Saml phys
   Ofc 1612 Corinthia Dr Samo 345-2221
   Res 218 Prospect Pl Cmrn 287-6264
Atwood Harry T & Eleanor K
   80 Battle Bridge Rd Mlvl 382-8219
Auber Brian 39 North St Samo 345-3621
Auber Susanna 75 Cameron Av Cmrn 287-4200
Aubin Wm 555 Conestoga Ct Samo 345-8130
Aubrey Guy & Fran 2 Park Ln Hunt 256-3327
AUDET REAL ESTATE
   1800 Millville Rd Mlvl 382-7730
Austin Bruce D vetnarn
   222 W Colchester St Jtown 333-2828
   Res Farmview Rd Samo 345-5522

Austin Jos J 563 Fourth St EndJ 372-3735
Austin Oscar & Meg 76 Sand Av Wyby 244-7728
Austin Wayne V 25 Plains Rd Cmrn 287-9872
AUTO PARTS PLACE Bugbee Ter Wyby. .244-6632
Auto Shop Old Forge Rd EndJ. 372-8817
Automotive Supplies & Service Inc
   55 S Union Av Jtown 333-7718
AVERY RENT A CAR
   Local Reservations & Information
     Municipal Airport 333-2727
   Worldwide Reservations & Info
     Tulsa Okla
     Toll Free—Dial '1' & Then 800-331-1212
Avon Agatha 700 Floodgate Rd Samo 345-8219
Avon Janet & Edgar W
   15 Riveredge Pl EndJ 372-5516
Avon M C 709 Sunset Ter Wyby 244-7729
Azar Khaled 235 Main St Mlvl 382-1182
Aztec Corp 1 Pendergast Rd Jtown 333-9876
BJ's Variety Store 45 River Rd Samo 345-3829
BTU Energy Resources Inc
   200 Sand Pit Rd Jtown 333-0287
   Evenings Sun Holidays 333-2425
Babcock Carolyn (Geo Mrs)
   4900 Cathedral Sq Jtown 333-4473
Babcock Carolyn 10 Oak Ln Jtown 333-4827
BAKER'S DOZEN bakery
   58 Roosevelt Rd Mlvl 382-8281
Balloon Bouquets Nationwide
   Toll Free—Dial '1' & Then 800-534-7000
Ballou Chas Y 54 Seville Ct Hunt 256-0870
Bonkowski Igor 12 Trailer Pk Mlvl 382-2827
Bourey Donald 69 Standish Rd Wyby. 244-8419
Bygone Days antiques
   Main Mall Jtown 333-1776
Cameron Community Church
   Fairfield Av Cmrn. 287-6662
   Logan John T Rev 13 Main St Cmrn 287-1726
CAMERON TOWN OF
   Cameron Free Library 287-4424
   Fire Dept
     To report a fire Cmrn 287-5511
     Highway Dept Foster Rd 287-8172
   Police Dept Foster Rd 287-7754
     Cameron Av station 287-1817
     For All Emergencies Only 911
     For All Other Purposes 287-2700
   School Dept
     John F Kennedy Elem School. 287-7756
     Cameron High School. 287-2177
   Town Hall Mountain St 287-6666
   Youth Office 261 Concord Rd. 287-8190
CAROUSEL DANCE STUDIOS
   122 Hadley Av Jtown. 333-8008

Carson Clancy J Insurance
   2910 Morgan Horse Rd Wyby 244-5537
   2910 Morgan Horse Rd Wyby 244-6885
   Res 10 Tabor Ct Mlvl 382-8531
Carter Chas & Mary 23 Mill Rd Cmrn 287-7863
Carter Geo D 67 Bellevue Dr Mlvl 382-9675
Carter Karen & Tim 12 Grant Pl Hunt. 256-8839
Carter Lee G optmtrst
   60 Seminary Rd Jtown 333-7721
   Res 75 Poker Table Dr EndJ 372-1726
Cartier Alphonse 5 Bayview Av Hunt. 256-8544
Cartland J Norman 98 Pine St Wyby 244-7728
CARUSO CANDY CO
   Main Mall Jtown 333-2222
   Evenings .333-6472
Cary Edw atty 45 Fletcher Rd Hunt 256-8117
Cary Ethel CPA 242 Broad St Jtown 333-8906
Cary Nan & Jack 80 Hickory Dr Mlvl 382-1176
CASA ROMANO RESTAURANT
   100 Livermore Rd EndJ 372-1235
CAVANAUGH—see also Kavanagh
Cavanaugh Felix 907 Larime Cir Hunt 256-8007
Cavanaugh Jas phys 20 Benn Av Mlvl 382-5527
Cavanaugh Wm & Maria 9 Park Pl Cmrn . .287-4133
Cavanaughs Liquor 10 School Rd Wyby . . .244-5552
Caycedo Paul archt 8 Quarry St EndJ 372-6029
Cedar Ridge Camp Ground
   Jamestown Park & Recreation 333-6565
CENTRAL BUS LINES
   Terminal
     Fare & Schedule Information
       1300 Main St Jtown. 333-4455
     Package Express & Baggage
       1300 Main St Jtown. 333-1281
CENTRAL STATE PUBLIC SERVICE CORP
   Jamestown Area
     Bus Ofc Randall Rd Jtown 333-8008
     Line Supt Ofc 333-2727
     If No Answer At Above Numbers
       Toll Free—Dial '1' & Then . .800-664-3344
   Huntington Area
     Bus Ofc 400 Huntington Pk 256-8281
     Line Supt Ofc 256-1821
     If No Answer At Above Numbers
       Toll Free—Dial '1' & Then. . . .800-869-5885
Conklin, Thos dent 30 High St Wyby 244-7284
Consolidated Cleaning Service
   Millville Mall 382-3627
Conti Mario 33 North Av Cmrn 287-9037
Continental State Bank
   200 Central Av Jtown. 333-3627
   1 Constitution Square Hunt. 256-6663
   7200 Samoset Blvd Samo 345-7728
Damico Jody 15 Highgate Av Hunt 256-9002
D'Amico Joe D 245 Pond Rd Mlvl 382-3728

The yellow pages in a telephone directory give the names, addresses, and telephone numbers of businesses and professional people. They are listed under the name of the kind of business or service they are. Some businesses and services also advertise in the yellow pages.

The Yellow Pages

Directions: Work with a partner and use the telephone directory yellow page listings to answer these questions. Notice that the names of towns are abbreviated. A key to the abbreviations is on the telephone directory page.

1. If you want the names and telephone numbers of drugstores, where must you look in the yellow pages? _____

2. You want to take dancing lessons. What is the address and telephone number of the Jamestown Dance Studio? _____

3. What are the two locations of the Continental Dance Academies? _____

4. What is the name of the public library in Jamestown? _____

5. Is the Ho-Hum Motel in Cameron or in Waybury? _____

6. What is the name of the pharmacist at Wesley Drugs? _____

7. What is the telephone number of Global Airways? _____

8. What is the address of the ABD Auto Repair Shop? _____

9. Is there a motel in Millville? _____

10. What kind of books does the Frayed Page sell? How do you know? _____

Now make up questions of your own. Ask your partner to answer them or have a different student answer each one. Use your telephone directory yellow pages if possible. Otherwise use the listings provided. Write your questions on a separate piece of paper.

Town Abbreviations and Exchange Numbers

Cmrn = Cameron	287	Hunt = Huntington	256	Samo = Samoset	345
EndJ = Enders Junction	372	Jtown = Jamestown	333	Wyby = Waybury	244
		Mlvl = Millville	382		

▶ Aircraft Instruction

Flightmaster Inc
Municipal Airport Jtown 333-4487

▶ Airline Companies

Accent Travel Inc
1182 Charter Rd Cmrn 287-2000
95 Railroad Av Hunt 256-8372
Icarus Air Service (Charter flights only)
Municipal Airport Jtown 333-7575
Global Airways
Reservations & Information
Toll Free—Dial '1' & Then 800-510-5000
Air Freight
Municipal Airport Jtown 333-2918
Irving Airlines
Chicago Ill 800-443-4455
please see our display ad this page
WorldWide Airways
Reservations & Information
Toll Free—Dial '1' & Then 800-776-2244

▶ Athletic Goods
See Sporting Goods

▶ Attorneys
See Lawyers

▶ Automobile Body Repairing & Painting

ABD Auto Repair 12 Main St Hunt . .256-7362
Alpha Auto Hospital
515 Riveredge Blvd Cmrn 287-1514
please see our display ad this page
Harry's Body Shop 522 Lester Samo 345-8372
Triangle Repair High St Jtown 333-4882
Xpert Kar Kare West Rd Mlvl 382-2091

▶ Automobile Renting

ARS/Auto Rental Service
Municipal Airport Jtown 333-2918
Old Mill Rd Mlvl 382-8888
256 Station Rd Hunt 256-1918
Miser Rent-A-Car
4050 Airport Blvd Jtown 333-1263
please see our display ad this page
Value Rent-A-Car
Municipal Airport Jtown 333-5252
please see our display ad this page

▶ Book Dealers–Retail

Book Place The 10 Kemper Rd Wyby .244-3832
Jamestown Book Shop
790 Shenanigan Dr Jtown 333-7734
please see our display ad this page

▶ Book Dealers–Used & Rare

Antiquarian Books Inc
26 S Manchester Blvd Wyby 244-8059
Frayed Page The 12 Sunset Dr Samo 345-9281

▶ Book Printers
See Printers–Book

▶ Book Publishers
See Publishers–Book

▶ Dancing Instruction

Continental Dance Academies
330 Memorial Dr Samo 345-8171
1162 Nicholas Av Jtown 333-7229
please see our display ad this page
JAMESTOWN DANCE STUDIO
* Ages 4–10: Creative Dance & Basic Gymnastics
* Ages 10 thru teens: Ballet & Jazz, Beginner thru Advanced
* Adults: Dance Conditioning, including ballet, modern, jazz & yoga
* Directed by Marietta Glockenspiel
2244 S Main St Jtown **333-9101**

▶ Drive-It-Yourself Automobiles
See Automobile Renting

▶ Driving Instruction

A-1 Automobile Driving School
500 Williams Rd Samo 345-8822
Master Drivers 4 High St Hunt 256-9382
Safety Auto School
Washington & Main Sts Wyby 244-1865
please see our display ad this page

▶ Driving Schools
See Driving Instruction

▶ Druggists
See Pharmacies

▶ Libraries Public

Cameron Free Library Main Cmrn .287-4424
Enders Junction Free Library
Railroad Av EndJ 372-8555
Huntington Memorial Library
Elmwood Pky Hunt 256-2560
Gage Memorial Library
Ash St Jtown 333-9281
Millville Town Library Court St Mlvl 382-1122
Samoset Village Library
Oak St Samo 345-2271
Waybury Local Town Library
32 Washington St Wyby 244-8376

▶ Motels

Ho-Hum Motel 55 Ortzen Rd Wyby .244-7763
Manasquan Manor-by-the-Sea
4200 Benn Av Cmrn 287-8130
Oak Tree Inn & Motel
200 Landers Dr (near mall) EndJ 372-5678
Restful Nite Inn Aichele St Samo 287-8112

▶ Opticians

Carter Lee G 60 Seminary Rd Jtown . .333-7721

CONTACT LENS CENTER
Eyes Examined—Contact Lens Service
Dr. Lester Rice & Dr. Mary Parsons
56 Columbia Cir Jtown 333-4949

Samoset Optical Inc
200 Marketplace Sq Samo 345-5678
please see our display ad this page
Steinberg Walter J optmtrst
262 Baxter Dr Cmrn 287-9382

▶ Pharmacies

City Pharmacy 291 Brood St Hunt . .256-3828
Dexter Drug Store 1 Day Rd EndJ . .372-9182
Hippocrates Pharmacy & Sundries
100 Constitution Rd Jtown 333-6363
Wesley Drugs 200 Station Rd EndJ . .372-4322
please see our display ad this page

*The community services pages in your tele-
phone directory tell you where you can get help
or information of various kinds. Look at the
listings below to see some of the kinds of things
you may find in your community services pages.*

Community Services Numbers

• •

Directions: Use the community services numbers to answer these questions. Work with a partner and be ready to discuss your answers with other classmates.

1. If you wanted information about services for blind people, what number
would you call?

   _____

2. Your elderly mother lives alone and
is at home, recovering from an opera-
tion. You want a nurse to visit her
occasionally. What number might
you call?

   _____

3. Your friend's uncle has decided he
wants to learn how to read and write
English. What number should you tell
your friend to call?

   _____

4. A married friend of yours wants to
meet with other young parents to talk
about raising their children. What
number should he call?

   _____

5. There's a serious flood in your town,
and people need immediate help in
this crisis. What number can you call
for disaster relief?

   _____

6. Your neighbor's little girl accidentally
swallowed rat poison. What number
can you call for help immediately?

   _____

7. Oscar becomes violent when he drinks.
a) What number should his wife call
when he becomes violent? b) What
number should Oscar call for help
with his alcoholism?

   a. _____

   b. _____

8. The Special Olympics will be held in
Jamestown next year, and you would
like to volunteer your services for this
event. What number should you tele
phone?

   _____

9. Someone is dumping chemicals into
the river in your town. What number
should you call to report this?

   _____

10. Your friend, out of work for three
months, wants to know the address
and telephone number of the State
Job Service. Can you help her?

   _____

Now make up questions of your own to ask a partner or the class. Use your own telephone directory community services pages if possible. Otherwise use the listings provided. Write your questions below.

_____

_____

_____

_____

_____

_____

_____

CONSUMER PROBLEMS

If your problem involves a specific business, always call their customer relations person first. If you are not satisfied, look among the listings in this category for the agency to help you:

Automobiles
Dealer complaints, see "Consumer Protection" below
Recalls, safety questions
   toll free 1-800-424-9393
Registry of Motor Vehicles
   Jtown 333-4600 Wyby 244-8059
   Safety Inspection Div Jtown 333-4604

Banks
Federal Savings & Loan, Fed Home Loan Bank
   Jtown 333-5300
National, Regional Admins of Nat'l Banks Jtown
   333-2274
State Chartered, Div Banks & Loans Jtown 333-2102

Business Evaluations
Better Business Bureau Jtown 333-9151

Consumer Protection, *to file complaints*
Atty Gen Ofc Jtown 333-8400
Waybury Consumer Advisory Comm
   Wyby 244-5505

Electric Companies
See "Utilities" below

Food & Drug
Federal Jtown 333-5860
State Hunt 256-2670

Gas Companies
See "Utilities" below

Hospitals
Div Health Care Standards Hunt 256-5138

Mail Fraud
Postal Inspector Jtown 333-7287

Product Safety
Consumer Product Safety Commission
   toll free 1-800-696-2772

Utilities
Contact company's Customer Service Dept. If problem is still not resolved, call Consumer Div, Dept Public Utilities: gas, electric, telephone and water
   toll free 1-800-192-6066

CRISIS
(available 24 hours)

Suicide/Personal Crisis
Crisis Clinic Jtown 333-3587

Alcohol/Drugs
County Counseling Svc
   Wyby 244-7641
Crisis Clinic Jtown 333-3587

Child Abuse
State Mental Health Svcs
   Hunt 256-0400
Spectrum Jtown 333-7429

Disaster Services
Red Cross Jtown 333-4581

Family Violence Program
County Counseling Svc
   Wyby 244-7641
Crisis Clinic Jtown 333-3587
Spectrum Jtown 333-7429

Poison
The Poison Center
   Cmrn 287-0222

Rape
Crisis Clinic Jtown 333-3587

CHILDREN & YOUTH

Child at Risk Hotline
   toll free 1-800-192-5200
Parental Stress Line
   toll free 1-800-132-8188

DISCRIMINATION

State Comm Against Discrim (SCAD)
   Jtown 333-3990

EDUCATION

Adult Basic Education
   Millville High School 382-8189
Learning Ctr 20 Prince Wyby 244-8761
University Extension Svcs
   244 Jamestown Rd Jtown 333-4452

EMPLOYMENT

Employment & Training Dept
   Federal Unemployment Compensation
      Jtown 333-2887   Samo 345-9918
   State Job Svc
      200 City Hall Jtown 333-2899
Occupational Retraining Center
   187 Hastings Rd Wyby 244-9620

ENVIRONMENT

Agriculture & Conservation Board
   66 City Hall Jtown 333-2918
County Environmental Protection Svc
   10 Sergeant Dr Hunt 256-2717
Greenpeace 80 Sky Rd Jtown 333-2867
Regional Planning Commissions
   70 City Hall Jtown 333-8918

FAMILY PLANNING & SERVICES

Family Education Center
   120 Highgate Rd Mlvl 382-9874
Mental Health Svcs, See Health & Mental Health
Planned Parenthood Jtown 333-4928
State Children's Aid Society
   5029 Burnside St Hunt 256-8762
Young Parents Program Wyby 244-2382

HANDICAPPED

Assn for the Blind Samo 345-8867
Assn for Retarded Citizens
   75 City Hall Jtown 333-2877
State Special Olympics
   toll free 1-800-879-4569
State Vocational Rehabilitation
   125 City Hall Jtown 333-2874

HEALTH & MENTAL HEALTH

County Health Council Samo 345-8530
Financial Programs
   Medicaid Jtown 333-2029
   Medicare
      local calling area Jtown 333-2035
      All other areas
         toll free 1-800-662-1111
Mental Health Svcs
   Alcohol & Drug Abuse
      79 City Hall Jtown 333-8997
   County Counseling Ofc
      17 Weller Rd Hunt 256-8817
Visiting Nurses Assn
   Memorial Hospital Wyby 244-9715

Answer Key

Page 27 Crossword Puzzles—The Calendar

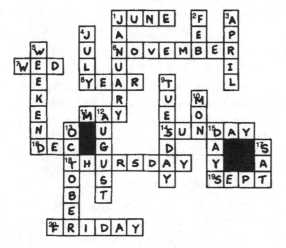

Pages 28 Crossword Puzzles—Countries, Nationalities, and Languages

Pages 30 Crossword Puzzles—Tag Questions

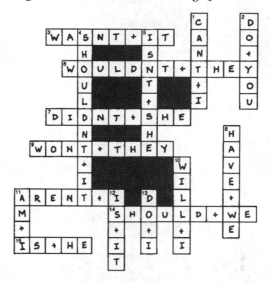

Pages 32 Crossword Puzzles—Irregular Verbs 1

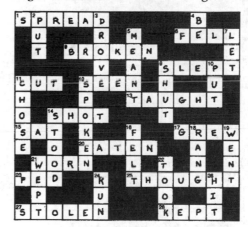

Pages 34 Crossword Puzzles—Irregular Verbs 2

Pages 36 Crossword Puzzles—Two-Word Verbs

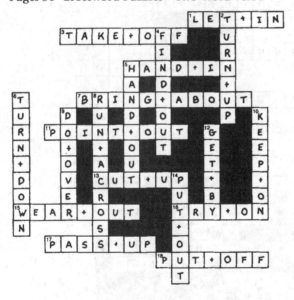

Pages 38 Crossword Puzzles—
Who Murdered Mrs. Van Tingle?

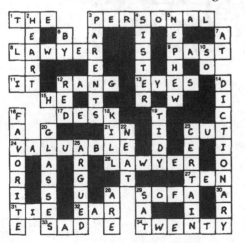

Pages 41 Crossword Puzzles—Comparisons

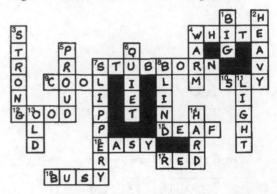

Page 44 You Be the Judge—
Mr. Brown and Mrs. Green

This case was brought to a New York court in 1955. The children's names were not changed. The judge said: " Children can never be embarrassed or confused by the name of their loving father. Nothing is stronger for their character or emotional security than to identify with a father who loves them."

Page 45 You Be the Judge—Bus Fare

This case was brought to a Missouri court in 1952. Mrs. Jones was awarded $1500. The judge said that the bus company should have adapted to "modern economic conditions" and have been prepared to change a five-dollar bill. A five-dollar bill is "no longer regarded as a bill of so large a denomination that it is unreasonable to require that change be given for it," the judge said.

Page 46 You Be the Judge—To Be in Miami

This case was brought to a Florida court in 1959. Max lost. The court ruled that a property owner cannot require his neighbors to build in such a way as to avoiding casting shadows on his or her land.

Page 47 You Be the Judge—
The Case of the Unhappy Worker

This case was brought to a Michigan court in 1956. John collected his severance pay. The judge ruled that he had been fired. "To call it 'acceleration of the worker's departure',," he said, "confuses the actual termination of employment with the reason for its termination."

Page 48 You Be the Judge—To Pass or Not to Pass

This case was brought to a Georgia court in 1955. Mrs. Smith won. The judge said that once the truck driver chose to signal Mrs. Smith to pass, he was obligated not to guide her into an accident. The driver was wrong and his employer had to pay the damages.

Page 50 It's Only Logical—Halloween Party

Arthur: Superman
Billy: the robot
Charles: the ghost
David: Mickey Mouse

Page 51 It's Only Logical—The Library Fire

Fire Chief: box of matches
Police Chief: rubber hose
Officer Grey: piece of cloth
Officer Black: gasoline can

Page 52 It's Only Logical—The Van Astorbilt Jewels

The pearl necklace was from Sylvester.
The gold bracelet was from Cyrus.
The ruby earrings were from Jonathan.
The emerald ring was from Waldo.

Page 53 It's Only Logical—A Busy Schedule

On Monday, Maria will go shopping.
On Tuesday, she'll clean the house.
On Wednesday, she'll take her parents visiting.
On Thursday, she'll wash the clothes.
On Friday, she'll work at the Child Care Center.

Page 54 It's Only Logical—Making the Grade

Bertha got a B.
Celeste got a C.
Esther got an A.
Maria got an F.
Pauline got a D.

Page 72 Using the Telephone—Long Distance

1. a. $1.52   b. 61¢   c. 92¢
2. 84¢
3. a. 307   b. 505   c. 207
4. a. 415   b. 509   c. 210
5. 613
6. a. 8:00   b. 6:00   c. 7:00
7. It's 3¢ cheaper to call Seattle. ($1.29 vs. $1.32)

Page 74 Using the Telephone—The White Pages

1. 100 Livermore Road, Enders Junction
2. 333-1281
3. No, only in Jamestown
4. 333-2425
5. 1-800-936-3837
6. 95 Railroad Avenue; 256-8217
7. Oscar

8. 45 River Road, Samoset; 345-3829
9. Yes. 7200 Samoset Boulevard
10. She's an attorney.

Page 76 Using the Telephone—The Yellow Pages

1. Look under *Pharmacies.*
2. 2244 South Main Street, Jamestown; 333-9101
3. 330 Memorial Drive, Samoset;
   1162 Nicholas Avenue, Jamestown
4. Gage Memorial Library
5. Waybury
6. Juan Rodriguez
7. 1-800-510-5000
8. 12 Main Street, Huntington
9. No, none are listed.
10. Used and rare books. It is listed under this heading.

**Page 78 Using the Telephone—
         Community Services Numbers**

1. Association for the Blind, 345-8857 (Listed under *Handicapped.*)
2. Visiting Nurses Association, 244-9715 (Listed under *Health and Mental Health.*)
3. The Adult Basic Education Program, 382-8189, is probably the best number to call first. The Learning Center, 244-8761, and the University Extension Service, 333-4452, might also offer adult ESL classes. (Listed under *Education.*)
4. Young Parents Program, 244-2382. He could also call Family Education Center, 382-9874. (Both listed under *Family Planning and Services.*)
5. Red Cross, 333-4581 (Listed as a *Disaster Service* under *Crisis.*)
6. The Poison Center, 287-0222 (Listed under *Crisis.*)
7. a. Look in *Crisis* under *Alcohol/Drugs* and *Family Violence Program*

   Crisis Clinic, 333-3587—for immediate help.

   County Counseling Office, 244-7641—for long-range help. Also Spectrum, 333-7429.

   b. Uncle Oscar could call the *Crisis* numbers under *Alcohol/Drugs* (see above). He could also look under *Mental Health Services:* Alcohol and Drug Abuse, 333-8997.

8. State Special Olympics, 1-800-879-4569.
9. County Environmental Protection Service, 256-2717. (Listed under *Environment.*)
10. State Job Service: 200 City Hall, Jamestown, 333-2899. (Listed under *Employment.*)

Index